UNDERSTANDING EUROPE

UNDERSTANDING EUROPE

by

CHRISTOPHER DAWSON

SHEED AND WARD

NEW YORK — 1952

PREFACE

THE average European has never given much thought to the nature of the international society to which he belongs. He has been taught to concentrate his attention on the history of his own nation and the political and economic problems of his own state. And so today, when the European question has become a vital political issue and the very existence of Europe is at stake, he is often at a loss to say what Europe is, what right it has to exist and what are the conditions of its survival.

Thus there is an urgent need for the better understanding of Europe, not only as a living society of peoples but as the creator of what we call "modern civilization". For however uncertain the political prospects of Europe may be, the overwhelming importance of its contribution to civilization remains, and unless we understand this, we cannot understand much about the world in which we live.

At the present time we are witnessing a sharp reaction against the world expansion of the European culture which took place in the last century. Yet even this reaction, paradoxical as it may seem, is a result of European influence, since Oriental nationalism and communism owe their origins to the transmission of Western ideas and Western political movements to the Eastern peoples.

In the same way it is impossible to understand the nature of European nationalism, unless we study it in relation to Europe as a whole, for Europe is essentially a society of peoples and it is through the co-operation and conflicts of the European nations that the characteristic achievements of European culture have been made.

v

Finally, we cannot begin to understand Europe itself unless we study the tradition of Christian culture, which was the original bond of European unity and the source of its common spiritual aims and its common moral values.

In the following pages I have attempted to study these three interrelated themes: that Europe is a society of peoples; that Europe is a spiritual unity, based on the tradition of Christian culture; and that the modern revolt against Europe is the inevitable result of its loss of the common spiritual aims and the common system of moral values which it derived from the Christian tradition.

Whether my readers agree or disagree with my conclusions, I think there are few who will deny that these questions deserve more attention than they have hitherto received, or that our system of education should give a larger place not only to the history of Europe but still more to the study of Christian culture.

ACKNOWLEDGMENTS

The author wishes to express his gratitude to the editors of the *Dublin Review*, the *Month, Lumen Vitae* (Brussels) and *Our Culture*, in which portions of this book have already appeared.

He also wishes to acknowledge his indebtedness to Geoffrey Bles Ltd. for permission to quote an extract from Nicholas Berdyaev's *The Origin of Russian Communism*: and to Baroness Budberg for an extract from her translation of *Fragments from My Diary* by Maxim Gorki.

CONTENTS

PART I: THE NATURE OF EUROPE

PART II: THE PRESENT CRISIS OF WESTERN CULTURE

PART I
THE NATURE OF EUROPE

CHAPTER I

How to Understand Our Past

N O ONE can look at the history of Western civilization during the present century without feeling dismayed at the spectacle of what modern man has done with his immense resources of new knowledge and new wealth and new power. And if we go back to the nineteenth century and read the words of the scientists and the social reformers or the liberal idealists and realize the mood of unbounded hope and enthusiasm in which this movement of world change was launched, the contrast is even more painful. For not only have we failed to realize the ideals of the nineteenth century, we are all more or less conscious of worse dangers to come—greater and more destructive wars, more ruthless forms of despotism, more drastic suppression of human rights. It is no good going on with the dismal catalogue, we know it all only too well. There is no need to listen to the alarmist predictions of writers like George Orwell or Aldous Huxley: it is enough to read the newspapers to convince ourselves that the cause of civilization is no longer secure and that the great movement of Western man to transform the world has somehow gone astray.

Whatever may be the ultimate cause of this crisis, it is certain that it is a spiritual one, since it represents the failure of civilized man to control the forces that he has created. It is due above all to the loss of common purpose in Western culture and the lack of a common intelligence to guide the new forces that are changing human life. Yet this failure is certainly not due to the neglect of education in modern society. No civilization in history has ever devoted

3

so much time and money and organization to education as our own. And it is one of the most tragic features of the situation that our failure has been the failure of the first society to be universally educated, one which had been subjected to a more systematic and completely national education than any society of the past.

In spite of this, there is no doubt that the modern European and American system of universal education suffered from serious defects. In the first place, the achievement of universality was purchased by the substitution of quantitative for qualitative standards. Education was accepted as a good in itself and the main question was how to increase the total output: how to teach more and more people more and more subjects for longer and longer periods. But in proportion as education became universal, it became cheapened. Instead of being regarded as a privilege of the few it became a compulsory routine for everybody. It is difficult for us to imagine the state of mind a man like Francis Place, labouring to all hours of the night after a hard day's work, out of sheer passion for knowledge.

In the second place, the establishment of a universal system of public education inevitably changed the relations of education to the state.

It is this above all else which has caused the mind of our society to lose its independence, so that there is no power left outside politics to guide modern civilization, when the politicians go astray. For in proportion as education becomes controlled by the state, it becomes nationalized, and in extreme cases the servant of a political party. This last alternative still strikes us here in England as outrageous, but it is not only essential to the totalitarian state; it existed before the rise of totalitarianism and to a great extent created it, and it is present as a tendency in all modern societies, however opposed they are to totalitarianism in its overt form.

For the immense extension of the scale of education and its ramification into a hundred specialisms and technical disciplines has left the state as the only unifying element in the whole system. In the past the traditional system of classical education provided a common intellectual background and a common scale of values which transcended national and political frontiers and formed the European or Western republic of letters of which every scholar was a citizen.

All the old systems of primary and secondary education presupposed the existence of this intellectual community which they served and from which they received guidance and inspiration. The primary school taught children their letters, the grammar school taught them Latin and Greek, so that educated men everywhere possessed a common language and the knowledge of a common literature or two common literatures.

Now from the modern point of view this traditional education was shockingly narrow and pedantic. It was also useless, since it had no direct bearing on the life of the modern world, on the world's work and on the techniques of modern civilization. Therefore the nineteenth-century reformers insisted first that education should be widened to include the whole realm of modern knowledge, and secondly that it should be made practically useful in order to produce skilled technicians and trained specialists or research workers.

These two great reforms have been generally applied, not without success, all over the world during the last fifty or a hundred years. But what has been the result? The domain of universal knowledge is too vast for any mind to embrace, and the specialization of the technician and the research worker has become so minute that it leaves no common intellectual bond between the different branches of knowledge.

A Russian expert in applied research on plant biology, a French specialist in the history of the romance lyric, an English worker on atomic research, an American expert in social psychology—all these do not belong to any sort of spiritual community like the humanist republic of letters. They are just individuals with special jobs, and there is a much stronger bond between *all* the Russians and all the Frenchmen and so on, than between scientists as such or technicians as such. No doubt the discipline of scientific research does produce a common type of intelligence and even a common type of character, but so did the older professional disciplines, so that there is a considerable similarity between staff officers or drill sergeants in the armies of the different great powers. But a similarity of this kind on the level of technique does not necessarily make for a similarity on the level of culture. And the same holds good for the scientific specialist. Indeed under present conditions the two types are rapidly becoming assimilated, so that the scientific expert and the military expert are alike instruments of the unified power organization of the modern state.

Up to a point this is inevitable, granted the complex nature of the modern scientific and technological order. But if it is allowed to develop uncriticized and unchecked, it is fatal to the old ideals of Western culture as a free spiritual community. It leads to the totalitarian state, and perhaps even beyond that to the completely mechanized mass society, to the Brave New Worlds and the nightmares of scientific utopianism in reverse.

How is it possible to preserve the guiding mind of civilization and to salvage the spiritual traditions of Western culture?

The philosopher, the religious leader, the statesman and the educationist all share this responsibility—all have a part to play. But the responsibility of the educationist is perhaps the most immediate and the heaviest of all, because it is in the sphere of education that the immediate decisions must be taken which will determine the outlook of the next generation.

In the past, as we have seen, education attempted to perform this higher function by means of the traditional classical discipline of humane letters—in other words of Latin and Greek. But we must be careful to distinguish between this particular form of higher education and higher education in general; and not to reduce the central inescapable problem to the old controversy between conservative classicism and radical modernism. It is quite possible that the traditional form of classical education has become completely antiquated and can no longer provide the universal unifying element which our civilization requires. But the fact that classical education no longer fulfils that purpose does not mean that civilization can dispense with such a unifying element altogether or that it can be found on a purely technological level.

On the contrary we need it more than ever before—and the more widely we extend the range of education, the more necessary it is to provide some principle of cohesion to counterbalance the centrifugal tendencies of specialization and utilitarianism.

Every form of education that mankind has known, from the savage tribe to the highest forms of culture, has always involved two elements—the element of technique and the element of tradition; and hitherto it has always been the second that has been the more important. In the first place education teaches children how to do things—how to read and write, and even at a much more primitive level how to hunt and cook, and plant and build. But besides all these things, education has always meant the initiation of the young into the social and spiritual inheritance of the community: in other words education has meant the transmission of culture.

Now the old classical education was a rather specialized and stylized type of this procedure. It took the tradition of humanism as embodying the highest common factor of Western culture and trained the young to appreciate it by an intensive course of philological discipline. At first sight it seems highly absurd to take an English farmer's son or the son of a German shopkeeper and drill him into writing imitation Ciceronian prose or copies of Latin verses. Yet for all that, it did set the stamp of a common classical tradition on a dozen vernacular European literatures and gave the educated classes of every European country a common sense of the standard classical values.

But it was only able to succeed in this specialized intellectual task because it was an intellectual superstructure that was built on a common spiritual tradition. Classical education was only half the old system of European education— below it and above it there was the religious education that was common to the whole people, and the higher theological education that was peculiar to the clergy, who provided the majority of the teachers in both the other departments of education.

Now the lowest level of this structure, which has been least studied and least regarded, was the most important of them all. It is true that it differed considerably in different parts of Europe, but for religious rather than material reasons. In Protestant Europe it was founded on the Bible and the catechism, whereas in Catholic Europe it was based on the liturgy and on religious art and drama and mime, which made the Church the school of the people. But in either case it provided a system of common beliefs and moral standards, as well as the archetypal patterns of world history and sacred story which formed the background of their spiritual world.

Thus considered as a means for the transmission of culture, classical education, important as it was, formed only one part of the whole system of social education by which the inheritance of culture was transmitted, so that even if it were possible to preserve or to restore classical education it would by itself prove quite ineffective as a solution for our present problem. What we need is not merely to find a substitute for the classical humanistic element in the old system; it is the system as a whole from top to bottom which has disappeared, and if the spiritual continuity of Western culture is to be preserved, we must face the problem as a whole and remember the importance of the common spiritual foundation on which the superstructure of higher classical education was built.

It is the failure to recognize this fact which has been largely responsible for the separation of higher education from its spiritual roots in the life of the people, so that our idea of culture has become a sublimated abstraction, instead of the expression of a living tradition which animates the whole society and unites the present and the past.

If we are to make the ordinary man aware of the spiritual unity out of which all the separate activities of our civilization have arisen, it is necessary in the first place to look at Western civilization as a whole and to treat it with the same objective appreciation and respect which the humanists of the past devoted to the civilization of antiquity.

This does not seem much to ask; yet there have always been a number of reasons which stood in the way of its fulfilment.

In the first place, there has been the influence of modern

nationalism, which has led every European people to insist on what distinguished it from the rest, instead of what united it with them. It is not necessary to seek for examples in the extremism of German racial nationalists and their crazy theories, proving that everything good in the world comes from men of Germanic blood. Leaving all these extravagances out of account, we still have the basic fact that modern education in general teaches men the history of their own country and the literature of their own tongue, as though these were complete wholes and not part of a greater unity.

In the second place, there has been the separation between religion and culture, which arose partly from the bitterness of the internal divisions of Christendom and partly from a fear lest the transcendent divine values of Christianity should be endangered by any identification or association of them with the relative human values of culture. Both these factors have been at work, long before our civilization was actually secularized. They had their origins in the Reformation period, and it was Martin Luther in particular who stated the theological dualism of faith and works in such a drastic form as to leave no room for any positive conception of a Christian culture, such as had hitherto been taken for granted.

And in the third place, the vast expansion of Western civilization in modern times has led to a loss of any standard of comparison or any recognition of its limits in time and space. Western civilization has ceased to be one civilization amongst others: it became civilization in the absolute sense.

It is the disappearance or decline of this naïve absolutism and the reappearance of a sense of the relative and limited character of Western civilization as a particular historic culture, which are the characteristic features of the present epoch. And at the same time we have begun to doubt the validity of the nationalistic approach to history and culture, and to realize the evil and folly of the blind sectarian feuds that have broken up the social unity of Christendom during recent centuries.

Thus it would seem as though the main obstacles to the understanding of Western civilization as a historic reality have begun to break down and the time is ripe for a new positive approach to the whole problem.

But there remains one serious obstacle—or rather there has arisen a new obstacle which was not present in the past. The events of the last forty years have inflicted such a blow to the self-confidence of Western civilization and to the belief in progress which was so strong during the nineteenth century, that men tend to go too far in the opposite direction: in fact the modern world is experiencing the same kind of danger which was so fatal to the ancient world—the crisis of which Gilbert Murray writes in his *Four Stages of Greek Religion* as "The Loss of Nerve".

There have been signs of this in Western literature for a long time past, and it has already had a serious effect on Western culture and education. This is the typical tragedy of the intelligentsia as shown in nineteenth-century Russia and often in twentieth-century Germany: the case of a society or a class devoting enormous efforts to higher education and to the formation of an intellectual élite and then finding that the final result of the system is to breed a spirit of pessimism and nihilism and revolt. There was something seriously wrong about an educational system which cancelled itself out in this way, which picked out the ablest minds in a society and subjected them to an intensive process of competitive development which ended in a revolutionary or cynical reaction against the society that produced it. But behind these defects of an over-cerebralized and over-competitive method of education, there is the deeper cause in the loss of the common spiritual background which unifies education and social life. For the liberal faith in progress which inspired the nineteenth century was itself a substitute for the simpler and more positive religious faith which was the vital bond of the Western community. If we wish to understand our past and the inheritance of Western culture, we have to go behind the nineteenth-century development and study the old spiritual community of Western Christendom as an objective historical reality.

The study and understanding of this cultural tradition ought to be given the same place in modern education as the study of the Graeco-Roman tradition received in the classical humanist education of the past. For the culture of Christendom is not only of vital importance to us genetically as the source of our own culture; it also has a greater intrinsic value than even the classical culture possessed. At first sight this may be questioned by the humanist, but I think that reflection will show that it is true even from the humanist point of view, for humanism itself as we know it is not the humanism of the Greeks and Romans, but a humanism which has been transmuted, if not created, by the Christian culture of the West. It is not merely that Erasmus and Vives and Grotius deserve our attention just as much as Quintilian and Cicero. It is that behind these men there is a living tradition, reaching back through Petrarch and John of Salisbury to Alcuin and Bede and Boethius, and it was this that built the spiritual bridge across the ages by which classical culture passed into the life of Western man.

The existence of this spiritual community or psychological continuum is the ultimate basic reality which underlies all the separate activities of modern Western societies and which alone makes Western education possible.

The obvious difficulty that has prevented the study of European culture becoming a part of the regular curriculum of studies is its vastness and its complexity. The great advantage of classical education was the fact that it involved the study of only two languages and two literatures and histories. But European culture has produced about twenty vernacular literatures, and its history is spread out among an even larger number of political communities. At first sight it is an unmanageable proposition and we can understand how educationalists have so often come to acquiesce in a cultural nationalism which at least saved them from being overwhelmed by a multiplicity of strange tongues and unknown literatures. But the true method, it seems to me, is rather to find the constitutive factors of the European community and to make them the basis of our study.

This means reversing the traditional nationalist approach which concentrated the student's attention on the distinctive characteristics of the national cultures and disregarded or passed lightly over the features that they shared in common. It means also that we should have to devote much more attention to the religious development, since it was in religion that Europe found its original basis of unity.

In the past there has been a tendency to treat political history and ecclesiastical history as self-contained subjects and to leave the history of religion to the ecclesiastical historians. But no serious historian can be satisfied with this state of affairs, since it destroyed the intelligible unity of culture and left the history of culture itself suspended uneasily between political and ecclesiastical history with no firm basis in either of them. It is essential to realize that the Christian community in the past was not a pious ideal, but a juridical fact which underlay the social organization of Western culture.

For more than a thousand years the religious sacrament of baptism which initiated a man into the Christian community was also a condition of citizenship in the political community. The obligations of Canon Law or Church Law were binding in a greater or less degree in Common Law, so that even in a Protestant land, like England, the fundamental questions of personal status and property—everything connected with the marriage contract and the right of bequest—fell within the purview of the Courts Christian.

The old English saying or legal maxim that Christianity is the law of the land faithfully reflects the situation which existed in Europe for a thousand years and more, from the time when the barbarian kingdoms first accepted Christianity. For this reception of Christianity was a solemn public act which involved the acceptance of a new way of life and a corporate adhesion to a new international community.

Now the comprehension of the nature of this sociological and psychological change is of much greater educational importance than most of the history that we were taught in our school and university days. This was a matter that we were supposed to learn from other sources. Whether we did so or not depended mainly on personal experience and family tradition.

Even today very little thought is given to the profound revolution in the psychological basis of culture by which the new society of Western Christendom came into existence. Stated in the terms of Freudian psychology, what occurred was the translation of religion from the sphere of the Id to that of the Super-Ego. The pagan religion of the Northern barbarians was a real force in society, but it was not an intellectual force and hardly a moral one in our sense of the word. It was an instinctive cult of natural forces which were blind and amoral, save in so far as war itself creates a certain rudimentary heroic ethos.

Now with the reception of Christianity, the old gods and their rites were rejected as manifestations of the power of evil. Religion was no longer an instinctive homage to the dark underworld of the Id. It became a conscious and continual effort to conform human behaviour to the requirements of an objective moral law and an act of faith in a new life and in sublimated patterns of spiritual perfection.

The sense of guilt was transferred from the corporate responsibility of the blood feud to the sphere of the individual conscience. It became the sense of sin and produced as a correlative, the act of repentance.

Now this spirit of moral effort and this consciousness of personal responsibility have remained characteristic of Western Christian culture—it may even be argued that they are its essential characteristics and that all its external political and material achievements have been to a considerable extent conditioned by them.

Of course it may be said that all civilizations are Super-Ego structures and that it is precisely this which distinguishes civilization from barbarism. But at the same time there are important differences in the part which religion plays in this process.

In some cases, as in Hinduism, the sharp breach with the forces of the Id which was characteristic of the conversion of the West has never taken place, and life is not conceived as a process of moral effort and discipline but as an expression of cosmic libido, as in the Dance of Siva.

On the other hand, in Buddhism we see a very highly developed Super-Ego. But here the Super-Ego is allied with the death-impulse so that the moralization of life is at the same time a regressive process that culminates in Nirvana.

No doubt similar tendencies were present in the Western world and find expression in the intermittent outbreaks of Manichaeism and other forms of religious and metaphysical dualism. But the characteristic feature of Western civilization has always been a spirit of moral activism by which the individual Super-Ego has become a dynamic social force. In other words, the Christian tradition has made the conscience of the individual person an independent power which tends to weaken the omnipotence of social custom and to open the social process to new individual initiatives.

At the present time historians and sociologists are no doubt inclined to minimize the effect of moral and religious idealism or conscious moral effort on the course of social development and to concentrate their attention on material motives; conflicts of material interests and the influence of economic forces. But whatever our ultimate religious and philosophical views may be, it is unjustifiable to rule out one series of historical factors, because we do not agree with the beliefs and ideals that are associated with them.

Take the case of modern Western colonial expansion. The historian and the sociologist have the right to dismiss the explanations of nineteenth-century imperialists with regard to the civilizing mission of the Anglo-Saxon race, and so forth, as an idealistic excuse to disguise the real facts of imperialist exploitation. Equally they have the right to regard the prospector or the trader as more genuine representatives of the colonial movement than the missionary or the educationalist. But they have not the right to deny the existence of the Western missionary movement as a real factor in colonial expansion, nor even to identify the two elements and to regard the missionary as an agent of capitalism with his collar turned back-to-front.

And the same principle must be applied to the history of Western Christendom in general. The historian may well argue that the feudal baron is more typical of mediaeval culture than the monk or the friar; he may equally point out how the Church became a stronghold of feudal privilege.

But he cannot deny that Christianity was one of the formative powers in mediaeval culture or that throughout the
whole course of Western history there was a spiritual élite
which was sincerely devoted to putting their ideals into
practice and making the Christian way of life a reality, while
at the same time the whole society was generally united in the
acceptance of Christian beliefs and in at least a theoretic
acceptance of Christian moral standards.

Now when these conditions have obtained over a continuous period of more than a thousand years, it is difficult to
deny that they must have had a great cumulative effect on
the life of Western man and the forms of Western thought
and feeling. Indeed it may be argued that Western culture
as a whole is the fruit of this thousand years of continuous
spiritual effort, and that there is no aspect of European
life which has not been profoundly affected by it.

If this is true, as I believe it to be, it seems to follow that
the history that we ought to study—the history that really
matters—is the history of this dynamic spiritual process,
rather than that of the conflicts and rivalries of the various
European states. But is such a study possible? The main
obstacle is certainly not lack of material—it is rather the
wealth of material which is still lying unused and sometimes
unknown. It is not so long ago that Henri Bremond wrote
his literary history of religious sentiment in France in the
seventeenth century, which even in its ten volumes is still
but a fragment of the work that he had planned. But even
so, he disclosed a whole new field of study of which even
specialists were largely unaware. And this is only one example of the rich mines of unused material for European
cultural history which lie, as it were, at our very doors.

No! The real difficulty that stands in the way of these
studies is an ideological or spiritual one, which affects the
very heart of the problem. If European culture is the

external expression of a dynamic spiritual process, how do we ourselves stand towards it? Are we part of that process or of some different process altogether? And is it possible to study the spiritual process of Western culture without taking sides one way or the other?

Now, in the first place, the acceptance of the Christian faith is not an essential condition for the study of Christian culture. It is perfectly possible in theory to appreciate and to study Western culture as a spiritual whole without being a Christian. That was, after all, the position of many of the great liberal humanitarian historians and sociologists of the nineteenth century. But these men never regarded themselves as outside the European tradition even in its spiritual aspect. They were very conscious of the moral dynamism of Christian culture and they accepted its ethos wholeheartedly. In fact they regarded themselves as having gone one better than their Christian predecessors by the attainment of a higher, purer and more sublimated ethical ideal. In short, they regarded themselves as super-Christians. Matthew Arnold is a typical example of this attitude, as we may see in *Literature and Dogma* or the preface to his *Irish Essays*. All this, however, has become a part of ancient history—an episode in an appendix to the process we have to study. The difficulty to-day is of a different nature.

We have to face the emergence of a more fundamental criticism of Christian culture which rejects its moral ideals and its psychological structure no less than its metaphysical theory and its theological beliefs. It involves the reversal of the spiritual revolution which gave birth to Western culture and a return to the psychological situation of the old pagan world, whether it takes the form of a conscious neo-pagan movement as with the Nazis, or some form of materialism which is equally opposed to the Christian world view. It is a revolt against the moral process of Western culture and the dethronement of the individual conscience from its dominant position at the heart of the cultural process. Consequently it means that the sense of guilt loses its personal character and is reabsorbed in the mass consciousness, reappearing not indeed in the old form of the blood feud, but in the parallel phenomena of racial hatred and class war, whereby the sense of guilt is extraverted and transferred to a guilty race or a guilty class which thus becomes a psychological scapegoat.

Now wherever this revolution has taken place there is no longer any room for the understanding of Christian culture. It simply becomes a question of *explaining away,* so that to the Nazi the achievements of Christian culture are explained in detail as examples of the Nordic genius asserting itself in spite of the obstruction of Mediterranean Christian and Semitic influences, while for the Marxian the history of Christendom must be rewritten in terms of the materialist interpretation of history, thus entirely altering the sense and direction of the movement of history.

The results of the new historiography may be seen in Rosenberg's *Myth of the Twentieth Century* or in the *Short History of the Communist Party of the Soviet Union,* which is perhaps even more significant, owing to its official and anonymous character.[1]

This psychological breach with the old European Christian tradition is a much more serious thing than any political or economic revolution, for it means not only the dethronement of the moral conscience but also the abdication of the rational consciousness which is inseparably bound up with it. It is indeed doubtful if Western society can survive the change, for it is not a return to the past or to the roots of our social life. It is too radical for that. Instead of going

[1] It was produced by a commission of the Central Committee of the C.P.S.U. but the authorship is usually attributed to Stalin himself.

downstairs step by step, neo-paganism jumps out of the top-storey window, and whether one jumps out of the right-hand window or the left makes very little difference by the time one reaches the pavement.

The alternative to this suicidal technique is to accept the existence of Christian culture as an objective historical fact and try to understand it by its own ideas and to judge it by its own standards, as classical scholars have done in the past with regard to the culture of the ancient world. For it is both unscholarly and unphilosophical to look at Byzantine culture through the eyes of the eighteenth-century rationalist, or mediaeval culture through the eyes of a nineteenth-century Protestant, or Christian culture in general through the eyes of a materialist.

Instead of these ways of looking at the past from outside as something alien, let us try to study Western Christian culture from the Christian point of view—to see it as a new way of life which was brought into Europe nearly nineteen hundred years ago, when St. Paul set sail from Troy to Macedonia, and gradually expanded until it became accepted as the universal standard of the European way of life.

This does not mean that we ought to ignore or slur over the gap between Christian ideals and social realities. On the contrary, the existence of this dualism created that state of vital tension which is the condition of European culture. In every age and every Western society this tension expresses itself in different forms, from the simple straightforward dualism of Christian culture and pagan barbarism which we see in Bede's *Ecclesiastical History* to the intense inner conflict "piercing even to the dividing asunder of soul and spirit" which we see in a Pascal or a Kierkegaard. Where this tension is absent,—where civilization has become "autarchic", self-sufficient and self-satisfied, there the process of Christian culture has been extinguished or terminated. But even to-day we can hardly say that this has happened. Indeed what we have seen during the last century has been something very different—an increase in spiritual tension which has become almost world-wide, although it has lost the positive element of religious faith that was an essential condition of its creative power in Europe in the past.

It is obvious that there is a profound difference between the old dualism of the Christian way of life and unregenerate human nature on the one hand, and the new dualism between the revolutionary ideas of liberalism, nationalism and socialism and the traditional order of society on the other, but there is a certain relation between the two, so that it is possible to maintain that the whole revolutionary tradition is a post-Christian phenomenon which transposes a pre-existent psychological pattern to a different sociological tradition. But even if that were the case, it would make it all the more important to understand how the archetypal pattern had originated.

We know as yet too little about the modern revolutionary social situation to understand it as a whole. But this is not the case with the ages of Christian culture that preceded it. Here the documentary evidence is more extensive than for any comparable period of world history. We know not only the course of its development from the beginning, we know the lives and thoughts of the men who played the leading part in that development from the beginning. We can study the development on every social and intellectual level from the highest to the lowest and in relation to all kinds of environments and social traditions.

It is from this development that the unity of Western culture is derived. For Europe is not a political creation. It is a society of peoples who shared the same faith and the same moral values. The European nations are parts of a wider spiritual society, and it is only by studying the nature of the whole that we can understand the functions of the parts. We have become so accustomed to studying the parts without reference to the whole that we are in danger of forgetting that there is any such thing as a cultural whole, a thing which the old classical humanist educators never entirely lost sight of, even when they seemed most pedantic. But this neglect of the study of our culture has been accidental rather than intentional—it resulted from a complication of different factors, some of which I have already discussed.

The time has come to repair this mistake. If we deliberately perpetuate it, now that we know what is at stake: if we consciously permit the guidance of the modern world to pass from the leaders of culture to the servants of power, then we shall have a heavier responsibility than the politicians for the breakdown of Western civilization.

No doubt there are very great practical difficulties in the way of a study which involves living religious issues as well as historical ones: difficulties as between Christians and non-Christians and still more between the adherents of the different forms of Christianity. But these difficulties are essentially practical, since none of the parties concerned— not even the non-Christians—is opposed in principle to the study of the Christian culture of the past as an objective historical phenomenon: indeed our own past is so deeply rooted in that culture that any refusal to study it means a refusal of history itself. Moreover, the field of work is so wide that there is ample room for all our schools of thought and all our social and religious traditions to follow their own lines of study without jostling one another.

In history as in other branches of knowledge there must inevitably be controversy and difference of opinion on a thousand particular points. But the justification of such conflicts is that they elucidate and do not obscure or obstruct. The essential task is to understand Christian culture as a whole arising from the impact of Christianity on classical culture and Western barbarism, and creating from these dissimilar elements a new spiritual world which forms the background of modern history.

For if we try to ignore or explain away this creative process in order to enhance the importance of our own national achievement or that of some contemporary political ideology, we deprive ourselves of our own cultural inheritance and narrow the intelligibility of history.

Such mistakes are possible—they have taken place in the past, and in so far as they have occurred they mark the great set-backs in the history of civilization. It is one of the greatest tasks of education to prevent this happening and to keep alive the common tradition of culture through the dark ages, or the periods of sudden catastrophe, when mass opinion is under the influence of passion and fear and when the individual has become the slave of economic necessity.

CHAPTER II

Europe and the Seven Stages of
Western Culture

THE existence of Europe is the basis of the historical development of the modern world, and it is only in relation to that fact that the development of each particular state can be understood. Nevertheless it is a submerged reality of which the majority of men are only half conscious. For the last century and more, the whole trend of education and politics and public opinion has tended to develop the consciousness of nationality and to stress the importance of the nation-state, while leaving Europe in the background as a vague abstraction or as nothing more than a geographical expression. The main reason for this is, of course, the cult of nationalism which, owing to its double appeal to political passion and to cultural idealism, exerts an exceptionally strong influence in the popular mind. But behind this there is a further cause which has not perhaps been sufficiently recognized. This is the tradition of education which has provided the framework of Western thought, and in this tradition the conception of Europe has never held a definite place. On the one hand, there was the history of the ancient world—of classical Greece and Rome—which was regarded as an essential part of education: on the other, and on a very much lower plane, there was the history of a man's own country and people, which every educated person was supposed to be familiar with but which did not possess the same prestige as classical history or humane letters or even natural science. A transition from one to the other was provided by such works as Gibbon's *Decline and Fall of the Roman Empire,* and it was books of this kind, which were the nearest approach to a study of Europe that the old tradition of education provided. But they were obviously partial and unsatisfactory, so that the consciousness of Europe as an historical reality was something which somehow had to be picked up on the road that led from ancient Rome to modern England (or whatever one's country might be), and it was only an exceptionally enterprising mind which troubled to enquire where and how it made its first appearance and what was its essential character.

From this defect in our education all modern culture has suffered. In fact the bitter harvest we are reaping to-day was in large measure the fruit of this initial error.

To ignore Europe and to concentrate all our attention on the political community to which we belong, as though it were the whole social reality, leads in the last resort to the totalitarian state, and National Socialism itself was only this development carried out with Germanic thoroughness and Prussian ruthlessness.

The democratic states have, on their part, no doubt refused to accept the extreme consequences of the nationalist heresy. They have preserved some contact with the tradition of Natural Law and a real sense of international obligation. Yet they also have ignored the existence of Europe as a social reality and oscillated between the reality of the nation-state and the ideal of a cosmopolitan liberal world order which was theoretically co-extensive with the human race, but was in practice dependent on the economic realities of international trade and finance. Yet apart from Europe, neither the one nor the other would have existed. For Europe is more than the sum of the nations and states of the European continent, and it is much more than a subdivision of the modern international society. In so far as a world society or a world civilization can be said to exist, it is the child of Europe, and if, as many peoples believe to-day, this ideal of world civilization is being shipwrecked before it has achieved realization, then Europe remains the most highly developed form of society that humanity has yet known.

What then is Europe? Europe is a community of peoples who share in a common spiritual tradition that had its origins three thousand years ago in the Eastern Mediterranean and which has been transmitted from age to age and from people to people until it has come to overshadow the world. The tradition as a whole cannot, therefore, be strictly identified with the European continent. It has come into Europe and has passed beyond it, and what we call "Europe" in the cultural sense is really only one phase of this wider development.

As I have argued in the previous chapter, we can only understand Europe and its historical development by the study of Christian culture, for this forms the centre of the whole process, and it was as Christendom that Europe first became conscious of itself as a society of peoples with common moral values and common spiritual aims.

Viewed from this centre, the whole development of Western culture falls into three main stages—Christian, pre-Christian and post-Christian, each of which may in turn be divided into two or three subordinate phases.

There are first the two phases of classical Mediterranean culture: (1) Hellenism and (2) the Roman world. Next there are the three central periods of Christian history; (3) the formation of Western and Eastern Christendom; (4) Mediaeval Christendom, from the eleventh to the fifteenth century; and (5) the age of religious division and humanist culture, from the sixteenth to the eighteenth century. Finally, we have (6) the age of Revolution—the later eighteenth and the nineteenth century, when European culture became secularized, and (7) the disintegration of Europe, which is both the cause and the result of the two World Wars in whose shadow we live to-day.

1. The first of these three stages is pre-Christian and even pre-European, since it originated in the Aegean and remained to the end a predominantly Mediterranean development. But it was emphatically Western, and all the later stages of European culture have looked back to it as the source of their intellectual and often of their social traditions.

For Western civilization was born when the Greeks first became conscious of their separation from the Asiatic world at the time of the Persian war, when they realized that they possessed a different way of life and a different standard of values from those which were embodied in the great archaic civilizations of the ancient East. These new ways of life and thought were already fully manifested in the great creative achievement of Hellenic culture during the seventh and sixth centuries B.C., the age that saw the development of the city-state and its political institutions, the great colonial expansion of the Greeks round the shores of the Mediterranean and the Black Sea, and the origins of the Greek scientific and philosophical movement. But during this earlier period the Ionians and the other Greeks of Asia Minor were the leaders of Hellenic culture, and European Greece held a relatively inferior position. The wars with Persia changed all that, not only by securing the European leadership of the Greek world, but still more by increasing the self-consciousness and unity of the whole Greek world against the oriental world empire that threatened its independence. For in spite of the jealous regionalist patriotism of the Greek city-states, they also acquired an intense loyalty to the wider unity of "Hellenism", so that the dualism of state and culture which was a characteristic feature of

mediaeval and modern Europe already finds its prototype
in the Greek world.

Thus the two poles of Greek civilization were the free
city and the common culture. It was as "free men", as
members of a self-governing community, that the Greeks
felt themselves to be different from other men, and it was
as members of the wider society of Hellenism which embraced a hundred cities and was in contact with every
part of the Mediterranean world that they developed their
co-operative work of thought and rational enquiry which
was the source of Western philosophy and science. In the
same way, they developed their own distinctive system of
education—*Paideia*—which was essentially different alike
from the traditional learning of the oriental priest and from
the warlike discipline of the barbarian tribesman and was
the origin and pattern of the Western tradition of liberal
education. In short, it was the Greeks who created the
Western idea of Man and that conception of humanist
culture which has become one of the formative elements in
the European tradition.

But though the Greeks were the real creators of the
Western tradition, they had little direct influence on continental Europe. The second great wave of Hellenic expansion
and colonization which began in the fourth century was
directed to the East, and during the Hellenistic period
Western and Central Asia, from the Mediterranean to the
Oxus and the Indus, was covered by a network of Greek
cities under the protection of the Graeco-Macedonian dynasties, which regarded the extension of Hellenic culture as the
basis and justification of their power. Thus Hellenism
became a real world-wide civilization which influenced the
culture of all the peoples of Asia as far east as North-West
India and Turkestan. But this movement of imperial expansion in the East was accompanied by the decline of Greek

power in Europe itself, and the same age that saw the conquest and Hellenization of the East by Alexander and his successors witnessed the rise of a new power in the West which was destined to act as the intermediary between the Hellenistic civilization of the East and the barbaric peoples of Western Europe.

2. This process forms the second phase in the history of Western culture. It covers a period of six or seven centuries—three hundred years from Alexander to Augustus and three hundred years from the death of Augustus to the conversion of Constantine, During those centuries Rome gradually grew from a peasant state in Central Italy to a world empire which embraced the whole Mediterranean world and extended from the Atlantic to the Euphrates and the Caucasus, and from the Rhine and the Danube to the Sahara and the Arabian desert. Thus for the first and last time in the history of Western culture the whole civilized world east of Persia and India was united in a single state ruled by one master, administered by a common law and defended by a uniform military system. At first sight there seems little in common between the Roman spirit and that of Hellenic culture. The Romans were a people of soldiers and organizers, lawyers and engineers, road-makers and land-surveyors, whose achievement is summed up in the lapidary sentence "Balbus built a wall". They had none of the genius for abstract speculation and the creative artistic imagination of the Greeks, and their vast empire, built up by harsh military discipline and ruthless political planning, seems as inferior to Periclean Athens as the Colosseum is inferior to the Parthenon. Nevertheless their work was extraordinarily enduring, and it served the cause of Western culture better than the more spectacular achievements of Alexander and his successors. While the latter were content to conquer the civilized East and cover it with a veneer of

Hellenistic urban culture, the Romans drove their roads like a plough through the virgin soil of Western Europe and laid the foundation of new cities where none had stood before. Though they were not the creators of Western culture they diffused and defended it, and the walls that Balbus built on the Northumbrian moorland and round the posts in the Libyan desert were the shield which protected the westward advance of the classical Mediterranean culture. The Greeks themselves, like Polybius and Strabo, were the first to recognize the nature of the Roman achievement as the indispensable continuation and completion of the achievement of Hellenism.

Thus the second phase of Western culture was in fact a co-operative effort which was common to the two great Mediterranean peoples. The Roman genius built the fabric of civilized society in Western Europe which still subsists to-day, at least in Italy and Gaul and Spain, in spite of the changes of later centuries. But this social order provided a channel for the transmission and diffusion of the Hellenic traditions. Latin literature and education as represented by Cicero and Livy, Horace and Quintilian, represent a simplified version of Hellenistic culture which was better suited to the needs of the new peoples of the West than the Greek original. Thus Latin endured as the common language of the educated world in the West for more than a thousand years after Greek ceased to be the common language of the civilized East. The strength of the Latin element in Western culture is no doubt due as much, or more, to the influence of the Catholic Church as to that of the Roman Empire. For the Church came to the Western barbarians with all the prestige of Latin culture and Roman authority. As Rome had acted as the intermediary between Hellenism and the West, so the Church acted as intermediary between the Latin West and the new peoples of Northern Europe. The last service which the Roman Empire performed in the development of Western culture was to provide the sociological and juridical basis for the organization of the new religious society with its ecclesiastical hierarchy and its Canon Law.

This task was only achieved by a long and costly struggle. Christianity is the one element in Western culture which is completely non-Western in origin, and which transplanted into the Roman-Hellenistic world a sacred tradition of immemorial antiquity, preserved intact by the one people that had held out indomitably against the pervasive influence of Hellenistic world culture.

Christianity came out of this unknown oriental world into the full light of Roman-Hellenistic culture with a new faith and a new standard of spiritual values which aspired to change human life and inevitably aroused the opposition of Greek culture and the persecution of the Roman state. In a single generation it spread from Syria through the cities of Asia Minor and Greece to Rome itself, and then proceeded, rapidly in the East and much more slowly in the West, to permeate the whole civilized world. For three centuries it had to fight for its existence, until it was finally recognized as the universal religion of the world empire. In the Eastern Mediterranean it maintained this position for more than a thousand years, but in the West it was hardly established before the Empire broke up under the pressure of the barbarians. Nevertheless the Western Church was strong enough not only to survive the fall of the Empire, but also to maintain the tradition of higher culture and to become a city of refuge for the conquered peoples.

3. The formation of Western Christendom by the conversion of the barbarians and the transmission to them of the tradition of Mediterranean culture by the Church marks a new stage in the Western development and the birth of the

new European society of nations. It was a slow process, since it was interrupted in the ninth century by a fresh wave of barbarian invasion from the north and the east and by the Moslem conquest of Spain and the Western Mediterranean, so that it was not completed until the Vikings of Scandinavia and the Magyars of Hungary had been converted and brought into the society of Christian Europe. But during these five or six centuries the foundations of a new Christian society were firmly laid by the co-operation between the Catholic Church and the barbarian kingdoms and by the missionary activity of the Irish and Anglo-Saxon monks, whose foundations were the centres of Christian culture and education in lands where no city had ever existed.

The focus of the new European development during these centuries was the Frankish kingdom, which included the greater part of France, Belgium and Western and Central Germany. This was the formative centre towards which the living forces of Western culture converged and in which the first deliberate attempt was made to realize the social unity of Western Christendom. This unity was based on the alliance of the new Frankish dynasty of the Carolingians with the Papacy, an alliance which was consummated and consecrated by the coronation of Charlemagne as Emperor at Rome on Christmas Day, A.D. 800. But it was primarily the work of the reforming party in the Church, as represented above all by Anglo-Saxon missionaries and scholars like St. Boniface and Alcuin. It was their ideals which inspired the new Carolingian legislation and the far-reaching programme for the revival and reform of learning, liturgy and script. All these activities were dominated by the conception of Christendom as an all-embracing unity which was both Church and state and in which the ruler had a sacred character as the anointed leader of the Christian people.

This conception survived the political collapse of the Carolingian Empire, which broke down under the stress of the Viking and Magyar invasions. It was inherited by the new society which grew up from its ruins;—the new Empire that was founded by the Saxon Kings of Germany in the tenth century, the feudal states that made up the Kingdom of France, and even by the Anglo-Saxon Kingdom of England which was founded by King Alfred and his successors. Mediaeval Christendom was in a real sense an extension and fulfilment of the Carolingian Empire and culture.

4. During these formative centuries, Western Europe had remained a relatively backward area on the extreme frontier of the civilized world. It occupied less than a third of the European continent and was by no means the richest or the most civilized part. But in the eleventh century Western culture began to expand from its Carolingian nucleus in all directions, and during the next three or four centuries it transformed Europe from a barbarian hinterland into a centre of world culture which equalled the older oriental civilizations in power and wealth and surpassed them in creative energy. These centuries saw the rise of the European city and the European state; they created a new art, a new poetry, a new philosophy, as well as new social, cultural and religious institutions: the order of chivalry, the estates of parliament, the religious orders and the universities.

All this cultural activity was inspired by the Carolingian conception of Christendom as a social unity, the society of the Christian people, which included and transcended the lesser unities of nation and kingdom and city. But this conception now found its primary expression, not in a universal empire but in the universal order of the Church as reorganized by the reforming movement of the eleventh and twelfth centuries. The Pope took the place of the Emperor as the head of the international society of Christendom and the ruler of the Christian people.

It is true that the Carolingian ideal of a universal Christian empire still survived, and even in the fourteenth century it was strong enough to inspire the work of the greatest of mediaeval poets—Dante. But by this time it was little more than a utopian ideal, whereas the international authority of the Papacy was a reality embodied in the law and institutions of Christendom and enforced by an effective system of centralized control. Thus mediaeval Christendom during its central period, from the time of Gregory VII to that of Boniface VIII (c. 1075–1300), was a kind of theocracy in which the whole social hierarchy of Christendom was dominated by the authority of the spiritual power.

This theocratic internationalism manifests itself in almost every aspect of mediaeval culture—in the crusades which were, at least in theory, international enterprises against the common enemies of Christendom; in the religious and military orders which were the international organs of Christendom; in the universities, like Paris and Bologna, which were international centres of higher studies for the whole of Western Europe. Moreover, the unity of European culture was reinforced by the use of Latin as the sacred language of the liturgy and the common language of learning, by the symbolism and imagery of a common religious art, and by the common ideals and conventions of aristocratic behaviour embodied in the cult of chivalry.

All these influences extended far beyond the frontiers of the Latin South and the Carolingian West. For it was during these centuries that Central and Eastern Europe as far as Poland and Lithuania and Hungary were brought into the society of Western Christendom.[1]

[1] Cf. Chapter v, *infra*.

But while this development was taking place in the West, the old centres of civilization in the East were beginning to decline under the pressure of new warrior peoples from the steppes. The Mongols destroyed the Bagdad Khalifate and conquered China, Persia and Russia, while the Ottoman Turks established themselves in Asia Minor and the Balkans and ultimately destroyed the Byzantine Empire. As a result of these changes, the axis of world culture gradually shifted westward, and the East began to lose its position of cultural leadership. Italy took the place of Greece as the most advanced country in Europe in art and learning and economic development. Indeed the city-states of Italy in the later Middle Ages rivalled those of sixth-century Greece in the intensity of their social and intellectual life.

5. At the same time, the progress of Western culture during the later Middle Ages was unfavourable to the unity of mediaeval Carolingian culture which was based on the alliance of the Papacy with the movement of ecclesiastical reform in France and Germany and with the ruling classes in the North which supported it and which also provided the driving force of the crusading movement. The renaissance of Mediterranean culture separated these elements, so that the reforming spirit which was still strong in the North became the enemy instead of the ally of the Papacy, while the latter became increasingly Italianized and was the leading patron of the new humanist culture. The theocratic unity of mediaeval Christendom was destroyed, and Europe became a society of sovereign states in which the temporal power of the prince either abolished or severely limited the spiritual power of the universal Church.

From the religious point of view this loss of Christian unity was a tragedy from which Christendom has never recovered. But it did not destroy the unity of European culture, since the influence of the new humanist culture which spread from Italy to the rest of Europe in the later fifteenth and the sixteenth centuries provided a bond of intellectual and artistic unity between the two halves of divided Christendom and between the sovereign states and nations of Europe.

Thus although Latin had ceased to be the common sacred language of liturgy and religion, it was more than ever the common language of education and learning. Moreover, the importance of the classical tradition in European culture was now reinforced and extended by the recovery of the Hellenic tradition, which from the fifteenth century onwards had an increasing influence on Western education and Western thought. This re-Hellenization of Western culture had its origins far back in the Middle Ages with the recovery of Greek science and philosophy from the Arabs by the translators of the twelfth century, and with the Aristotelian revival which had such a profound influence on Western thought in the later Middle Ages. But it was not until the Renaissance had restored a direct contact with Hellenic culture that the movement bore fruit in the great advance of scientific thought inaugurated by Copernicus and Kepler and Galileo. From the sixteenth century onwards Europe was to surpass the Greeks in the originality and boldness of its cosmological speculation. Every generation extended the boundaries of science, and Western man began to acquire a knowledge and control of nature which seemed to open unlimited possibilities of progress for mankind.

Meanwhile the external relations of European culture had already been profoundly changed. Before Western science had discovered the new world of knowledge, Western man had discovered and conquered a new geographical world. The defeat of the last crusades by the Turks at Nicopolis and Varna, and their control of the great historic trade routes to Asia and Africa, compelled Europe to seek new fields for expansion and new channels for trade. The maritime discoveries of the Portuguese in Africa which opened the new oceanic route to India and the Far East, and the discovery and conquest of the new world of America by the Spaniards, involved a general reorientation of Europe from the Mediterranean to the Atlantic and from the old continental trade routes to the new oceanic sea ways. The resultant development of economic activity and the oceanic expansion of European trade and colonization prepared the way for the world hegemony of Western civilization in the following age, but it also intensified the political rivalry of the European powers which was characteristic of this age and which was complicated by the religious conflicts of the post-Reformation period. The attempt to prevent this struggle for power from destroying the European state system led to the elaboration of the system of the Balance of Power, which was the product of Renaissance statecraft and reflects the tension of conflicting forces within the limits of a common culture. While the struggle for power was a revolutionary and destructive force, its agents were the most traditional and formal institutions in Europe—the courts of the great powers—which all tended to share in the same humanist culture and imitate the same patterns of social behaviour. Thus in spite of the disruptive effects of national rivalries, European war and diplomacy themselves produced an international society of a limited kind, so that Western statesmen and diplomats and generals during this period belonged to the same world and shared the same ways of thought and the same style of conversation and manners and dress.

6. This highly stylized aristocratic civilization of post-Renaissance Europe, which reached its full development in the age of Louis XIV, differed from the earlier phases of European development in its lack of religious foundations.

The stronger became the culture of the courts, the weaker became the culture of the Churches, so that by the eighteenth century European society began to undergo a process of rapid secularization which changed the whole character of Western culture. The alliance of the courts with the humanist culture and with the scientific movement which was still predominantly humanist in spirit generated the new ideals of enlightened despotism and of the rationalization of human life by the diffusion of scientific knowledge. The movement was strongest in France, where it possessed a consciously anti-Christian character and carried on a crusade of enlightenment against the dark forces of fanaticism and superstition which it saw embodied in the Church and the religious orders. From France the movement spread with extraordinary rapidity throughout continental Europe, using the courts and the aristocratic salons as its channels of diffusion, and extending even as far as Russia and Portugal.

Only in England did the movement take a different form. Here alone in Europe the court culture was relatively unimportant and the centre of power had passed to the great landowners who ruled the country through parliamentary institutions and were practically emancipated from royal and ecclesiastical authority. Under their rule, English society also underwent a process of secularization, but it was less complete and far less revolutionary than that of the Continent. The main energies of English society were directed to practical ends—to commercial and industrial expansion and to the revolution of economic life by capitalism and scientific invention. There was no sudden breach with religious tradition. Indeed in England, unlike the Continent, the eighteenth century witnessed a popular movement of religious revival which had a deep effect on the common people and the middle classes of English society. Thus in England the movement towards the secularization of culture followed a very uneven and irregular course. There was no sharp conflict between religious tradition and the scientific enlightenment, but a number of dissident sectarian or party movements which broke up the traditional unity of religion and culture and created their own separate creeds and ideologies.[1] Some of these movements, like the Unitarians, were in close sympathy with the Enlightenment and were led by philosophers and scientists like Joseph Priestley; others, like the Wesleyans, were inspired by the ideal of personal sanctity and evangelical simplicity. But they all acted, consciously or unconsciously, as a ferment of social change, and prepared the way for the reforming movements of the following century.

On the Continent, and especially in France, where these intermediate sectarian groups did not exist, the secularization of culture was far more complete, and the conflict between the movement of Enlightenment and the forces of tradition was far more acute. By degrees the Enlightenment became transformed into a kind of counter-religion, and the spiritual forces which were denied their traditional religious expression found their outlet in the new revolutionary cult which was embodied in the Declaration of the Rights of Man and was inspired by an irrational faith in Reason and by boundless hopes for the progress of humanity when liberated from the age-long oppression of priests and kings. Political democracy and economic liberalism were the practical corollaries of these beliefs, and the attempt to realize them by a drastic breach with the past and the introduction of new rational institutions led to the

---

[1] The foundations of this development had been already laid in the seventeenth century, in the age of the Puritan Revolution, and some of the seventeenth-century leaders like Roger Williams, the founder of Rhode Island, had already developed theories of the complete separation of Church and State.

French Revolution and the Reign of Terror and the Cæsarian imperialism of Napoleon.

The Napoleonic Empire was a bold attempt to re-establish the unity of Europe on new foundations, and for a moment it seemed as though a new Cæsar had arisen, capable of transforming the ramshackle edifice of the *ancien régime* into an ordered unity by his military genius and his powers of organization. But the classical symmetry of the *style empire* was little more than a plaster façade which hardly concealed the heterogeneous character of the underlying structure. There was an inherent contradiction between the military authoritarianism of the Empire and the liberal idealism of the Revolution, and the stubborn resistance of the two most independent Western peoples, the British and the Spaniards, ultimately aroused the dormant forces of European nationality and caused the downfall of Napoleon and the dissolution of his Empire. Nevertheless the revolutionary quarter-century from 1789 to 1814 had changed the face of Europe and the character of Western culture. It had swept away the venerable relics of mediaeval Christendom—the Holy Roman Empire, the territorial power of the Church with its ecclesiastical principalities and endowments, the hierarchical order of society and the sacred character of kingship. The *ancien régime* had suffered such a fall that all the powers of the Holy Alliance and all the statesmen of the Congress of Vienna were unable to put it together again.

In spite of all this, the work of the statesmen of Vienna was infinitely superior to that of their successors at Versailles in 1919 or at Dumbarton Oaks and San Francisco in 1944–45. For they faced the problem of European unity in a sane constructive spirit, without utopian illusions or nationalist prejudices. Their attempt to transform the old antagonistic principle of the Balance of Power into a prac-

tical system of international co-operation which was embodied in the Law of Treaties and the Concert of Europe
was fundamentally sound, and it gave Europe a longer
period of peace than it has ever known before or since.
Its failure was due not to any inherent defect, but to the
lack of any common spiritual principle strong enough to
overcome the centrifugal forces in European culture. The
revolutionary idealism which found expression in the secret
societies and in national liberalism and democratic socialism
was too strong to be restrained by the rigid conservatism
of the restored mónarchies. There was a glaring contrast
between the repressive traditionalism of the minor German
and Italian states and the immense progress of wealth and
population and scientific technique that was taking place in
the Atlantic world. Thus the new world of America became
the promised land of the European peasant and artisan;
and the balance between the two worlds was held by
England, the workshop and bank of the world, the ruler
of the seas and the home of parliamentary institutions.
This world-wide economic and colonial expansion of
Western culture, which was mainly the work of the two
English-speaking peoples, provided a safety valve for the
frustrated and repressed elements in Europe, like the
political refugees of 1848 and the far more numerous
victims of famine and industrial depression. But at the
same time it strengthened the centrifugal tendencies in
nineteenth-century culture, so that the expansion of Europe
was also a flight from Europe. In spite of the genuinely
pacific aims of the Vienna settlement and the Concert of
Europe, the Holy Alliance was everywhere regarded by
liberals and democrats as a conspiracy of kings against
peoples and of despotism against liberty.

Consequently at the very time when the external prestige
of European culture was at its highest and the world was

being conquered and transformed by European science and wealth and power, Europe itself was being torn asunder by the increasing violence of its internal conflicts. In England the bloodless victory of constitutional reform in 1832 inaugurated a long period of social peace and economic progress inspired by the ideology of Victorian Liberalism. But on the Continent the conflicting forces were too extreme and too evenly matched to admit of such a compromise. The traditions of revolutionary liberalism, nationalism, and social revolution all helped to undermine the restoration settlement and to destroy the Holy Alliance, but they were incapable of combining to create a new European order. The ultimate victor in the struggle was the centralized and militarized national state, like the new German Empire which represented an alliance between the old tradition of Prussian militarism and the new ideology of German nationalism. But neither of those elements was favourable to the ideal of European unity, and the Bismarckian era witnessed a spiritual decline of European culture which was in sharp contrast to the increasing economic power and military efficiency of the European state.

7. In the last period of our survey, from 1914 to 1950, this internal disintegration of European culture manifested itself in the new phase of war and revolution which has destroyed the European society of peoples and has deprived Europe of its world leadership.

During this period the threat of German military imperialism united the rest of the world against her and forced first Britain and then the United States to abandon their traditional isolation from continental Europe and to convert their economic and financial power to military ends. The result of the First World War was to destroy the three great military empires of Central and Eastern Europe and thus to clear the ground for a new social and political system.

But the attempt of the Western powers to reorganise Europe and the world on liberal democratic principles did not succeed in meeting the needs of the situation or controlling the revolutionary forces that had been released. On the ruins of the military empires there arose the new totalitarian states of Soviet Russia and National Socialist Germany, which alike by their conflict and their collaboration destroyed the emergent democratic national states of Eastern Europe and precipitated a Second World War.

This second war was even more disastrous in its effects on European culture than the first. Europe has been not only economically ruined and morally weakened; it has been cut in two by the new frontier between Western Europe and the Communist-controlled East. This frontier, which passes through the heart of Central Europe, is not merely a political boundary; it is a line of division between two alien worlds which excludes the possibility of social intercourse and cultural communication, so that the man who wishes to pass from one part of Europe to the other is forced to abandon his citizenship and become a fugitive and an exile. Thus the old European society of states, which even fifty years ago was still the focus of world power and the leader of world civilization, has become a truncated fragment too small and too weak to exist without the military protection and economic aid of America.

Must we conclude from all this that Europe no longer exists and that the problem of European unity is no longer relevant to the present situation? Not necessarily so, since the present division of Europe is so recent and so artificial that it is difficult to believe in its final character. But in any case it is impossible to exaggerate the seriousness of the present crisis both for Europe itself and for the world. The division and impoverishment of Europe must inevitably lead to the division and impoverishment of the world, for

Western Europe has played and still plays such an important part in world commerce and industry, and still more in science and thought, that its decay would inflict a more serious blow to world civilization than the fall of the Roman Empire or any other of the historic catastrophes which have caused the decline of some particular centre of higher culture. The very suddenness of the decline of Europe suggests that it may be a temporary crisis rather than a final catastrophe, since the fall of cultures in the past has usually been preceded, as in the case of the Roman Empire, by a slow process of decline and sterility lasting for centuries, whereas the present crisis of European culture took place when the social and economic activity of Western culture was at its highest pitch of development. It is due not to any decline of physical or social vitality, but to the internal division of Europe by an intensive process of revolutionary criticism which affected every aspect of Western culture. This process did not consciously aim at the destruction of European unity. At each successive stage it was inspired by a belief in social progress and the hope of a new European order. In fact the European revolutionary movement as a whole was not a symptom of social decadence, but an expression of the energy and optimism of an age of social and economic expansion. But the revolutionary ideal of a new European order was frustrated by the conflicting aims of the different revolutionary movements—liberal, socialist and nationalist—so that the revolutionary movement became destructive of European unity and hostile to European culture itself. In the bitter intensive struggle of parties and ideologies the deeper spiritual foundations of Western culture were forgotten or rejected until the movement which had begun with the worship of liberty and the Declaration of the Rights of Man ended in the concentration camps of the totalitarian state and the mass suicide of total war.

The process of European revolution has thus reached an absolute conclusion. There is no going forward on this path. If the peoples of Europe desire to survive, they must seek a new way. The age of revolution was also an age of world expansion when Europe was threatened by no external enemies, so that each of the great powers was a law to itself. During the last forty years this situation has been completely reversed and the peoples of Western Europe find themselves in a position of relative inferiority as a minority group exposed to the pressure of stronger and more united non-European world powers.

This catastrophic change must inevitably have a powerful effect on the immediate future of the peoples of Europe. But it may operate in two opposite directions. It may lead to discouragement, pessimism and despair, or alternatively it may make the European peoples realize their common interests and the need to restore the broken unity of European culture. If world expansion has led to cultural disintegration, then we might expect that external pressure would promote internal unity. But the essential problem is not the political issue of European federation or the practical question of European economic organization. The vital question is how to preserve the spiritual inheritance of Europe and restore a common purpose to Western civilization. The great world civilizations of the East were based on a sacred law of immemorial antiquity embodied in an unchanging pattern of institutions and customs. But Western culture has always owed its strength to the persistence of a dynamic purpose which has enabled it to change the world, to widen the frontiers of human knowledge and extend the range of human activity, without losing the continuity of its spiritual tradition and the community of its moral values. If this dynamic purpose can be restored, the spirit of Europe will survive and the unity of Western culture will reassert itself in some new form. For these fundamental issues belong to the plane of religion rather than to that of politics or economics, and these planes do not coincide. An age of material prosperity may often be an age of spiritual decline, while a dark age of material destruction and economic decline may see the birth of new spiritual forces.

CHAPTER III

Europe not a Continent but a Society of Peoples

THE question of the nature of Europe—of the relations of the European states to one another and of the parts to the whole—has always been the great problem in all attempts to establish an international order. But the concept of Europe has usually been taken for granted in international discussion. It is seldom defined, and when defined, it has usually been only in a superficial way.

In the past this did not matter, because the international community was regarded as practically identical with the European community, and the law of nations was in practice simply the body of rules which were commonly accepted by the states of Europe in their dealings with one another.

The situation changed gradually and almost imperceptibly during the nineteenth century—first by the rise of the United States and the independence of the states of Latin America, and secondly by the development of the international status of the independent powers of Asia and their conformity to European diplomatic usages. But Europe remained the centre and pattern for the international system, and when the League of Nations was founded in 1919 as a world organization, it was really not so much the creation of a new system as the completion of the process of European expansion and the application of the European international system to the rest of the world. But the Treaty of Versailles which inaugurated the League of Nations failed to establish European order. The old system of the Balance of Power and the Concert of Europe was abandoned, but there was no place in the new system for Europe as a society of peoples. Europe was no longer sufficiently united to lead the world, and the world was not sufficiently organized to impose order on Europe. And consequently, instead of being the organizing centre of world order, Europe became the focus of international disorder.

The Second World War, which was also a European civil war of unprecedented destructiveness and bitterness, has left Europe weaker and more divided than ever before. The leadership of the world has passed to the giant states of the non-European world—to the U.S.A., and the U.S.S.R.— and Europe occupies a position somewhat similar to that held by the Balkans in the later nineteenth century—a breeding ground of conflicts between the great powers and a dependent region to be organized and divided in rival spheres of influence.

In the new international organization of the United Nations which has taken the place of the old League of Nations, Western Europe has only 8 member states out of a total membership of 59. Thus it can be outvoted in the General Assembly not only by America with 22 votes and Asia with 16, but even by the Caribbean and Central American states alone, which number 10.

Nevertheless it is not possible to judge the importance of a culture by the artificial regulations of a temporary international organization, nor even by the material and military standards of power politics. For even to-day after the immense expansion and political advance of the non-European world which have changed the scale of our thought and altered the standards by which the statesmen and historians of the past reckoned, Europe still remains the greatest centre of world population and the richest and most highly cultured area in the world. It is also, in spite of its feuds and dissensions, the most interdependent and interrelated group of states that exists. Every European state depends on its neighbours to a degree that is unknown in Asia and Africa and which is only partially attained in America.

This diversity and interdependence of the European state system has always been an essential condition of European culture and the source of its strength as well as of its weakness. The basis of this diversity is to be found in the physical structure of Europe, which is a continent of peninsulas and narrow seas, where the land runs out into the Atlantic, and the Mediterranean and the Baltic penetrate into the very heart of the land. Geographically speaking, it is not a continent at all, but merely a peninsular extension of the great Eurasian land-mass. As we have seen, it is a man-made continent, an historical creation, an invention of the Greeks, who adapted a myth in order to express their sense of independence towards the civilization of Asia and their struggle for freedom against Persian imperialism.

And the same diversity which characterizes Europe as a whole is also characteristic of its parts. Europe is an extremely regionalist society, and almost every European country has only been unified with the greatest difficulty and usually in quite recent times. Take Yugoslavia—you have Croatia, Slovenia, Dalmatia, Bosnia and Herzegovina, Old Serbia, Macedonia, Montenegro—all with their separate characteristics and their strongly marked social personalities and historical traditions.

Take Spain—in the north alone you have Galicia, Leon, Old Castille, the Basque Provinces, Navarre, Aragon, Catalonia—half a dozen peoples speaking four different languages, with their own traditions of culture and even of separate political institutions.

Take Italy, which in its great days was a sort of miniature Europe—a society of states of the most diverse type divided by fierce political rivalries but united by a strong sense of common culture.

Take Switzerland—the oldest and perhaps the most successful federal state in the world, which grew out of the most diverse and apparently anarchic system of leagues and alliances and in which the cantons still retain their ancient tradition of autonomous life.

So it is throughout Europe—everywhere the tradition of independence and diversity and an intense development of regional life. It is not till we come to the sandy, featureless plain of North-East Germany that we find a different type of landscape and a different pattern of society, and thenceforth eastwards diversity yields to uniformity and the influence of the great central land-mass becomes more pronounced.

Thus old Europe, with all its faults, was a real society of peoples, and the status of the lesser states did not depend merely on their military and economic resources but on their historic rights and their cultural achievements. For in Europe the centres of power and the centres of culture did not necessarily correspond, and the key points of European social life were by no means concentrated in the great states. Thus for many centuries the main artery of European life was not dominated by any great state, but passed through a series of small independent states and confederations from the Italian city-states in the south to the United Provinces in the north, with the Swiss Confederation dominating the mountain barrier in the centre, which was of such vital strategic importance for the whole of Western and Central Europe. In the same way the cities that were most characteristically European, with the exception of Paris, were not the capitals of the great powers, but the independent or semi-independent centres, like Rome and Florence, Geneva, Zürich and Basle, Augsburg and Nuremberg, Ghent and

Bruges, Leiden and Amsterdam, Bremen and Lübeck, and, far to the east, Novgorod, the last representative of free Russia.

All this seems very remote from modern Europe, yet it is impossible to understand the nature of Europe unless we remember the existence of all these different strands from which the texture of our civilization has been woven. And this tradition of pluralism and diversity is still maintained in the Europe of to-day by the smaller states, which therefore represent a far more important element in European civilization than we can assess by material standards. Yet even when they are judged by material standards, the small states have proved their efficiency. Even the poorest of them, such as Bulgaria or Finland, were far richer and more prosperous in their independence than when they formed part of a great empire; while those which possess the longest tradition of freedom, such as Switzerland, the Netherlands, Norway and Sweden, have attained the highest standards of life in relation to their natural resources of any societies in the world.

When we turn to Eastern Europe, we find ourselves confronted with a totally different development, in which uniformity takes the place of diversity and the mass takes the place of the individual. But this development does not really form part of the European tradition, whatever its geographical position. Europe has never had an Eastern frontier. Like the Hellenic world it is a marginal development which has never flourished far from the sea. The nominal geographical boundary between Europe and Asia has never been a political or cultural or even a physical frontier. For example, the old Kievan Russia belonged to Europe, and Central Russia, the land between the Volga and the Oka, became part of Christendom in the tenth to the eleventh centuries. But on the other hand, the South

Russian and Bessarabian steppes belonged to Asia and remained the home of Moslem Tartar peoples right down to the nineteenth century. In fact, the South Russian steppe was colonized by Europeans at about the same time as Ohio, and Odessa is the contemporary of Cincinnati or Cleveland. A hundred years ago the two greatest states of Eastern Europe, Turkey and Russia, extended, one from the Danube to the Persian Gulf, the other from the Baltic to the Behring Sea. At that time, and throughout the period which preceded the crisis of the present century, there was a very sharp contrast and division between Eastern and Western Europe. The former was dominated by four military empires, superimposed on a mass of subject peoples and provinces, while the latter consisted of a large number of independent states which were for the most part constitutional monarchies and which were, or aspired to be, independent national states.

It has never been sufficiently recognized how much of our present problems arise directly from this situation. We cannot insist too often that the two World Wars, the failure of the League of Nations and the general collapse of European order are due not as the Marxians say to the inevitable consequences of the capitalist system, but quite simply and directly to this European dualism—to the breakdown of the four military empires in Eastern Europe and to the far-reaching changes involved in the construction of a new state system to take their place. This process of change reaches back to the Turkish Revolution of 1908 and the abortive Russian Revolution of 1905, and ever since then—that is to say, for forty years and more—Eastern Europe has been in a state of effervescence and change, with new states rising and falling and a continual change of frontiers until finally Western Europe, and ultimately the whole world, were drawn into the orbit of disturbance. I do not mean to say that capitalism (or better, the financial-industrial development of Western society) has no share in the catastrophe of our civilization, but its responsibilities have been in the sphere of culture. Left to itself, capitalism does not breed world war—indeed, where it has been most highly developed, in the U.S.A. and the British Empire, the economic rivalry it produces has been reconcilable with peaceful relations and even a considerable measure of mutual disarmament. The real source of world war has been the disintegration of the military empires—a disintegration which made them prefer the risks of war, to which they were accustomed, rather than the risks of political changes, which threatened the basis of their power and ultimately their very existence.

The fall of the empires produced two great changes. The first was the resurrection of the submerged nationalities of Eastern Europe, some of which like Poland and Bohemia had had a great history in the past, while others like the Finns, the Esthonians and the Slovaks were virgin peoples who had never before taken part as political entities in the society of European nations.

The second was the rise of the new type of mass state which we call totalitarian. This was due in part to the difficulty of adapting the forms of parliamentary democracy to the very different conditions of Eastern Europe and in part to the survival of the traditions of the old military empires in Eastern Europe and their re-adaptation to the circumstances of the new age.

For though these empires were from one point of view old-fashioned, cumbrous, out-of-date political organisms, they were, from another point of view, more adaptable to the requirements of state socialism and mass organization than the liberal democracy of Western Europe, created to meet the needs of a prosperous middle-class society which valued personal liberty, and private property and individual initiative above all else.

Thus the political evolution of Eastern Europe in the twentieth century proceeded apparently in two opposite directions. On the one hand, the old Ottoman and Austrian empires disappeared and their place was taken by small states, based on the principle of nationality, while on the other hand, the Russian and Prussian monarchies were transformed into great mass states which were stronger both internally and externally than the military empires that they replaced.

It was clearly impossible to reconcile these two contradictory lines of development with one another and with the conception of a European society of nations. After the first War the twelve or fourteen lesser states of Eastern Europe, however sharply divided by national rivalries, were as a rule sympathetic to the ideals of the League of Nations and were anxious to share in the general movement of European culture and to strengthen their political and cultural links with the peoples of Western Europe. But the rise of the totalitarian super-states destroyed the prospects of such a development before it could mature. The smaller peoples of Eastern Europe were ground to pieces between the upper and nether millstones of Communist Russia and Nazi Germany, and the whole international structure of Eastern Europe has been destroyed.

At the close of the last War, in the years of Yalta and Potsdam, it was often argued that this result was inevitable and that the smaller powers of Eastern Europe could only exist as dependents or satellites of a great power. But we have now learnt to our cost that it is difficult to maintain freedom in one part of Europe if we abandon it in another, and the incorporation of the whole of Eastern and East Central Europe in a single totalitarian power system has weakened and undermined the political structure of Western Europe also. For the small states play an even more important role in the political order of Western Europe than they did in the East. In pre-war Europe there were fourteen independent states in Eastern Europe exclusive of the U.S.S.R., and fourteen in the West exclusive of the German Reich; it is true that the Western states included three "great powers" in addition to Germany, with a population of over forty million apiece, whereas all the fourteen states of Eastern Europe, except Poland, were under the twenty-million mark. But though the small states of Western Europe were not quite so numerous as those of the East, they made up for this by the strength of their national consciousness and the importance of their contribution to European culture. It was in Western Europe that the smaller states first obtained a clear constitutional recognition of their rights in the society of nations, and the existence through so many centuries of states like the Swiss Confederation and the Kingdom of Denmark and the Netherlands, side by side with the great powers, is one of the most striking features of European culture.

No doubt the situation of the small state alike in the East and the West has been rendered difficult by the development of total war and totalitarian economic planning. But are the "great powers" themselves in a much stronger position? I mean the old Western European powers—as distinct from the totalitarian world states. England is to some extent untypical, owing to her links with the non-European world. But France, the classical example of the old type of Continental great power, shared the fate of Belgium and Holland and Denmark in 1940. And Italy, the equivalent power on the side of the Axis, proved to be equally insecure in 1944. It is only as part of a larger whole that the states of Western Europe can survive, whether they are great or small.

And so we come back to the starting point, that Europe is a society of peoples, and can only survive as such. If this idea was firmly implanted in the minds of statesmen and educated men and the men in the street, there would be more chance of its being realized. Unfortunately the whole weight of government propaganda and official history and politics has always been so concentrated on the ideology of the state and the nation, that the larger European unit has been left to take care of itself. Long before the Germans had invented their totalitarian conception of autarchy, European nationalism had an autarchic bias which made men neglect and undervalue the unitary aspects of European society except in so far as these could be viewed in an abstract and universal form.

Thus we see, on the one hand, an intense but narrow national state patriotism; on the other a broad, but rather abstract, internationalism—both alike characteristic products of European culture. In the past both these tendencies could co-exist with one another in the same country and even in the same individual, so that a somewhat unstable equilibrium was established. But in times of revolution and war this balance is destroyed and the abstract ideals of humanity and civilization are sacrificed to the interests of the sovereign state which is a law to itself. And consequently, after every great war we find efforts being made to establish some kind of supernational order which will replace abstract ideals by a legal or institutional system of relations. Thus after the Napoleonic wars we had the Holy Alliance with its strong insistence on European unity and solidarity and its neglect of the principle of nationality, while after the First World War we had the League of Nations which recognized the existence of a world-wide society of states, but did not find any place in its organization for that historic society of peoples which we call Europe.

So again to-day we see a fresh attempt to establish a supernational order on a world society of states in the United

Nations Organization which was created by the representatives of the fifty allied states assembled at San Francisco in 1945. But, as we have already seen, the European peoples have a smaller share in this organization than in any of its predecessors, and the existence of Europe as an organic society of nations is completely ignored. The United Nations is essentially a cosmopolitan organization: the organ of an ideal world community which does not as yet exist. It recognizes the rights of nationality and the claims of power, but takes no account of those historic societies of peoples which alone make the existence of an international order possible.

The true international position of any particular state in Europe does not depend merely on its military power or on its juridical status as a sovereign state, but on its historic place in the structure of European society and its partnership in the European cultural community. I mean that the relation of Norway to Denmark and Sweden cannot be compared with the relation between Norway and Saudi Arabia, or to that between Sweden and Afghanistan, though these are units of approximately the same population. It is an organic historic and structural relation without which these states would not be what they are.

The failure to recognize the importance of these organic cultural communities is the great weakness of all schemes of international organization that are based either on abstract rights and the equality of sovereign states or on purely material standards like size and population. The tendency of international law has been to conceive state sovereignty as a kind of juridical autarchy which was largely fictitious, but which was compensated by the existence of an elaborate network of diplomatic, economic and cultural relations through which the public life of Europe was actually carried on.

In the well-known, but not sufficiently well-known, passage in which Burke expounds his conception of the Commonwealth of Europe against the totalitarian tendencies of the French Directory in 1796, he distinguishes these three elements: in the first place the Law of Nations, which is "the great ligament of mankind"; in the second place the Law of Treaties, which is the public law of Europe; and finally "the Law of Civil Vicinity", the Law of Neighbourhood, which determines the rights and duties of states according to the situations in which they stand in relation to one another. This Law of Neighbourhood exists in nature and tradition and custom, but it has not hitherto received adequate recognition from the international lawyers and political theorists. Nevertheless it is on this that the very existence of the smaller states depends; and until we can regard states as neighbours within a local society as well as units in the balance of world power we shall not have created a civilized international order.

In the past the civilization which gave fullest recognition to this Law of Neighbourhood was that of ancient Greece, and it was to this that its great achievements were at least to some extent due. From the political point of view the behaviour of the Greek city-states was no less greedy and selfish and unscrupulous than that of any other states. Where they excelled was in their development of the cultural relations that united the states of each region and of the whole Hellenic world in a metapolitical community that even war and hostile political alliances could not destroy. Now the true nature of European unity is of a similar kind, and the states of Europe resemble the cities of Hellas rather than the racial empires of the East. It is true that the cult of nationality has tended for the last century and a half to accentuate the racial element in the European nations and to obscure or undervalue their community of culture. Pan-

Germanism, Pan-Slavism, Pan-Turanianism—all of them explicitly or implicitly deny the European community and turn their eyes back to the forest and the steppe. And so it is here that the small states have a special claim to speak for Europe, for it is their interest as well as their tradition to maintain the principle of the existence of free societies enjoying full rights as members of the European Commonwealth. And some of these states, notably Switzerland and the Netherlands, though they are far from being archaic survivals, are the direct descendants of historic groups of cities and provinces which developed, like the Greek city-states and federations, on the basis of the Law of Neighbourhood.

Hitherto the existence of this European Commonwealth of Nations has never been fully recognized or found any adequate institutional expression because it could not be squared with the two dominant political ideologies—the cult of the sovereign state and the ideals of cosmopolitan internationalism. But this is also true of the British Commonwealth of Nations, and the existence of the latter and its relative success in creating a society of self-governing states prove the possibility of an intermediate society between the extremes of the sovereign national state and the international world community.

The British Commonwealth is a kind of World State, since there is no quarter of the world and no continent in which it does not possess member states and vital interests. Yet is not a World State like the monolithic, totalitarian, autarchic, continental World States. It is the extreme opposite of these, since it has developed the pluralist and self-determining element to its extreme limits. We can say of it to-day what Burke said 150 years ago: "The British state is without question that which pursues the greatest variety of ends and is the least disposed to sacrifice any of them to another or to the whole."

Viewed from the standpoint of Roman Law and the classical theory of state sovereignty, it is difficult to see how the British Commonwealth can be regarded as a state at all. Yet it is a political reality and one which has solved some of the most difficult problems of political and international relations more successfully than either pure imperialism or pure nationalism has done.

Now it is clear that a state of this nature cannot fit into a world pattern of continental mass states. The small national state might continue to exist as a subordinate and regimented unit, but a state like the British Commonwealth could not survive at all. It is therefore just as much the interest of the British Commonwealth as it is the interest of the smallest states in Europe to build a world order which is not based on the power of a few mass autarchies, but on the rights of every society that possesses national consciousness and historical tradition. This is not yet fully recognized by public opinion, largely because the public opinion of the Commonwealth, as distinct from its member states, is so little developed. That is a defect that the British Commonwealth shares with the European Commonwealth, where, to a still greater degree, the part is everything and the whole is neglected. Nevertheless, the fact that it has been possible to build up a powerful political organism in which a number of peoples can attain national consciousness and free democratic institutions while preserving a common organization of law and mutual defence may be of decisive importance for the political development of the future. Ever since the Renaissance the political development of continental Europe has been dominated by a conception of sovereignty derived from Imperial Rome, which made the state an ultimate absolute irresponsible entity. Just as, in the eighteenth century, the petty princelings of Germany each attempted to make himself a miniature Louis XIV and to surround himself with all the pomp of a Baroque monarchy, so the modern national states have taken over the ideal of unrestricted sovereignty which had been formed by the absolute monarchies. But as sovereignty within the state has been transformed by the coming of democracy and the participation of the governed in the government, so also a democratic international order requires a revision of our conceptions of the external conditions of sovereignty which will render it possible to create true societies of states and commonwealths of nations.

The experience of the British Commonwealth has disproved the Hobbesian doctrine that if political power is not concentrated, society returns to the law of the jungle. It has shown that it is possible to divide sovereignty and yet preserve the bond of peace and the order of civilized community. Why should not this experience be applied by the peoples of continental Europe, who are even more conscious than we are of the inalienable rights of small nations and of the value of their contribution to culture? The failure of the European system has been primarily due to the unlimited and unrestricted development of the principle of sovereignty. So long as the great states based themselves on power politics and the law of the stronger, and the small states modelled themselves on the great states, a state of international anarchy was unavoidable. And so we had the strange spectacle of the most highly civilized society of states that has ever existed deliberately ignoring its civilization and reasoning itself back to the law of the jungle. There is, however, another and an older tradition than the Renaissance ideal of absolute sovereignty and rationalized power politics; it is the mediaeval conception of Europe as the commonwealth of Christian peoples: a single society, consisting of a diversity of peoples and states, bound together by a network of mutual rights and obligations and founded on a common spiritual citizenship and a common moral and intellectual culture. It seems to me that this tradition is not only higher, but also more true to historical and sociological realities, than the other. Its failure to influence events has not been due to its impracticable character, but to the fact that it has been ruled out *a priori* by the political philosophers as well as by the practical politicians. What it demands is what the world needs, namely that the peoples of Europe shall conduct their affairs like a civilized community, and not like a band of brigands, recognizing that their rights are not conterminous with their powers and that their duties to one another are no less morally and legally binding than their duties to their citizens.

Unfortunately, during the last two hundred years these ideas were usually confined to idealists who viewed political problems in an abstract and unhistorical fashion, so that public opinion, even educated opinion, was forced to choose between the power politics of an exclusive nationalism and the world plans of a rootless cosmopolitanism. Neither alternative admitted the existence of Europe or the value of those bonds between the nations which are so deeply rooted in the history of our civilization but which find no adequate expression in the political philosophy of the sovereign state. But here the example of the British Commonwealth is of inestimable value as supplying a middle term between these two extremes. For in some respects the British political tradition has been more conservative than that of the Continent, even where it has been more liberal. It has preserved important elements of the older European tradition that have been eliminated by the one-sided rationalization of the state and of the theory of sovereignty which developed on the Continent since the Renaissance. No doubt the British tradition has not been rational enough. It has developed in an instinctive and empirical fashion, and it has failed to give any adequate interpretation of its political practice which could be assimilated by other peoples. In fact, we have had no first-rate political thinkers since Burke, whose influence on the Continent was deflected by the polemical anti-revolutionary form in which his thought was expressed.

But it would be a great misfortune if the inarticulateness of the British Commonwealth should prevent its experience being considered in the ideological debate in which the future of Europe is at stake. Because our political tradition does not fit into the rigid scheme of state sovereignty which has been accepted alike by the anti-national imperialisms of the Continent and by the democratic nationalism, it is liable to be dismissed as camouflaged imperialism, and the possibilities of a genuine dual citizenship are ignored, although they have been actually realized for nearly a hundred years in our Commonwealth. Yet from the sociological point of view it is impossible to explain the facts of European life and culture unless we admit some such dual citizenship. The most typical representatives of our civilization—Erasmus, Leibniz, Goethe, for instance—were not primarily citizens of a particular state; they were citizens of Europe: and the states of Europe could never have become what they were had they not implicitly recognized that they formed part of a wider society. The weakening of this European consciousness has been one of the greatest weaknesses of the last hundred years, and if our civilization is to survive it must be reasserted in a more conscious and explicit form. The peoples of Europe must learn to take their European citizenship no less seriously than their national citizenship, and this is above all necessary for the smaller peoples who can no longer exist as isolated atoms in an international chaos.

It is on their co-operation and not on the military hegemony of a single power that European order must be based.

Hitherto European unity has always been conceived in terms of the concert of the great (and rival) powers or a military imperialism. But we have seen again and again that no solution is possible on these lines. Any state which attempts to dominate Europe by its own strength for its own interests ends by becoming the enemy of Europe, while the concert of the great powers becomes a euphemism for a diplomatic war of competing imperialisms in which the rights of the smaller peoples are used as counters in the game. The alternative of a European order based on the union or confederation of the smaller states has never yet been attempted or even regarded as within the bounds of possibility. But the events of the last years have changed all that. It is not merely the work of Versailles that has been destroyed. The whole international structure of nineteenth-century Europe to the Congress of Vienna and beyond has been swept away. The European order must be reconstituted on new foundations, and the corner-stone of this reconstitution must be the rights and responsibilities of the relatively small peoples, which form the most typically European social units and on which the future of European culture so largely depends.

CHAPTER IV

Germany and Central Europe

THE difficulties imposed on the European society of
peoples by the inadequacies of the European system
have nowhere been greater than in Central Europe,
above all in the German lands. Ever since the Middle Ages
Germany and Austria have been a kind of microcosm of
Europe—a society of peoples with a common culture, but
politically divided and continually disturbed by internal and
external wars. Moreover the two problems are so intimately
connected with one another that it is hardly too much to
say that the fate of Germany is the fate of Europe, and that
the very existence of Europe as an international society
depends on the solution of the German problem.

European opinion has always been more or less conscious
of this, and statesmen have again and again attempted to
make the reorganization of Germany the key to an international settlement of European problems. The attempt
was made in 1648 by France and Sweden in the Peace of
Westphalia, it was made by Napoleon in the Confederation
of the Rhine, it was made by Alexander I and Metternich
and Castlereagh at Vienna in 1814–15, and finally it was
made by the victorious Western powers at Versailles in 1919.
And on every occasion they have failed, because they have
attempted to solve the German problem in terms of the
Balance of Power and European security without taking full
account of the peculiar character of the German problem
and the historic forces that have conditioned it.

But the responsibility does not rest with the Western

powers alone. If Western statesmen have over-simplified the problem by subordinating the needs of Germany to the interests of Europe, the Germans have replied by an even more drastic simplification which subordinated the needs of Europe to the interests of Germany and imposed this one-sided solution by force of arms. Bismarck himself was a great simplifier who united Germany under Prussian leadership by the resolute and forcible exclusion of all those elements in the German and Central European traditions which were inconsistent with his conservative Prussian solution, while in our own days Hitler has brought ruin on Germany and Europe by the enormous and disastrous simplification of a "New Order" for Europe based on a totalitarian and racialist Germany party state. Under the circumstances it is not surprising that the victorious powers in 1945 concluded that international order could only be established by the complete elimination of Germany as an independent power centre. Yet it has only taken five years to show us how completely we were mistaken. The elimination of Germany has solved none of the problems of Europe. On the contrary it has involved the elimination of all the other independent powers in Central Europe and has increased the dangers of Western civilization to an appalling degree.

Geographical and economic conditions make it impossible to separate the fate of Germany from that of Central Europe, or that of Central Europe from the West. The idea, widely diffused in some quarters, that it is possible to reorganize the world round two world centres, based on the United States and the U.S.S.R., breaks down because it is impossible to draw a world frontier through one of the most thickly populated and highly organized areas in the world in defiance of economics, geography and culture. In spite of national conflicts, Central and Western Europe is a closely knit

economic whole, and it is impossible to eliminate and
segregate Germany without disrupting the whole European
economic system. The reconstruction of Europe—of the
European economy and the European social order—cannot
therefore take place without the active co-operation of Germany, and the problem we have to face is how to find a
political order which will make this co-operation possible.
But we cannot do so by transplanting Russian Communism
or Anglo-Saxon democracy to German soil, for even if it
were possible it would only provoke ideological conflicts
which would prevent international co-operation. Somehow
or other the elements of a new political order must be
found in the German tradition itself. No doubt there is a
large and influential body of opinion that would deny the
possibility of such a solution, on the ground that the German
tradition is directly and primarily responsible for the evils
of Nazism and all the disasters that Europe has experienced
during the last generation. But the fact that National
Socialism has deliberately exploited certain tendencies in
German character and tradition to almost insane extremes
does not prove that these are the only tendencies. On the
contrary, the violence of its excesses must provoke a reaction
in which it should be possible for the submerged elements
in the national tradition to reassert themselves.

Now in order to understand Germany, it is essential to
take account of the extreme complexity of its historical
development, and the disunity and multiplicity of its political
traditions. The relations between nation and state, between
government and society, and between culture and politics
were entirely different from what they have been in England
or France. In the west the development of national patriotism
and national culture went hand in hand with the development of a national state. Nation and state were comple-
mentary aspects of a single sociological process. But in

Germany the development of national consciousness and national culture has followed an independent course from that of the state and the political order. For upwards of six hundred years Germany was a society of states, a kind of miniature Europe with a common culture but no unitary system of political organization. It is true that the mediaeval Empire maintained a shadowy existence until 1809, and its successor, the Germanic Confederation, survived until 1866, but these were not national states, but loose interstate organizations comparable to the League of Nations on a smaller scale. Within these organizations there existed three rival Germanies, none of them fully national but each capable of becoming the basis of a national German state.

The first and oldest of the Germanies was the Germany of the west and south which had been the heart of the mediaeval Empire but which had long since lost all semblance of political unity. It was the most divided of all European lands, a rabbit-warren of petty principalities and a museum of archaic survivals. Yet this was the Germany which was most conscious of its common nationality and its common culture, and which at the same time was most internationally minded and shared most fully in the common traditions of Western culture. It was the Germany of Goethe and Schiller, of Weimar and Göttingen and Heidelberg. And it was also the homeland of the statesmen and men of action like Stein and Metternich and Hardenberg and Scharnhorst, who played the leading part in both Austria and Prussia during the early nineteenth century.

Closely united with this Germany by history and tradition was the great imperial state of Austria, which had inherited the prestige and the tradition of the Holy Roman Empire. In the course of centuries Austria had become a predominantly non-German empire, extending to the Carpathians and the Mediterranean and embracing half a dozen different nations and racial groups, Czechs and Magyars, Italians and Poles, Rumanians and Croats. But in spite of this it still preserved its links with Western Germany, and it was to Vienna rather than to Berlin that the lesser German states, and still more the German Catholics, looked for leadership and protection.

And finally there was Prussia, the new self-made power which had arisen from very humble origins in the course of a single century, until it had become one of the great military powers of Europe and the rival of Austria in the leadership of the Germanic Confederation.

This was the state which was the architect of German national unity and the creator of modern Germany by its military and political efficiency and by the genius of its soldiers and statesmen. Yet it was far from being a typical German state. From the standpoint of traditional eighteenth-century German constitutionalism it was not a German state at all, but a colonial Baltic power which had elbowed its way into Germany and established an alien despotism on the ruins of the Reich. Even in the nineteenth century, when Prussia had made itself the champion of national unity, there were many who looked askance at the Prussian achievement, and asked themselves whether the new Reich was not simply a Prussian empire which Prussia had built for her own profit and glory at the expense of greater Germany. No doubt this was a minority view, and the majority of Germans came to accept the Prussian version of German history established by writers like Droysen and von Sybel and Treitschke, who regarded Prussia as the embodiment of all that was best in the German tradition, and the new empire as the final and ideal solution of the German problem. And this view also found wide acceptance abroad, not least in England and America from the time of Carlyle onwards.

Nevertheless this view is just as one-sided as the minority view. In reality the Bismarckian solution was not a final one, but a transitory episode in an age-long process of change. The Second Reich was the *tour de force* of a political genius, and it did not survive for more than a generation after his guiding hand was removed. It was created by military power in the hands of a statesman, and it was destroyed by military power divorced from statesmanship. But the fundamental causes of its instability were its one-sidedness and the inherent discordance between the Prussian and the German traditions of culture.

Prussia is the most remarkable example in history of a state that was created artificially from above, by the government and the personal power of its rulers. Its real founder was neither the Great Elector nor Frederick the Great, but Frederick's father, Frederick William I, a man of limited intelligence and unattractive personality, who nevertheless achieved a kind of greatness by his stubborn unimaginative devotion to a single idea and a single technique. On the idea of universal state service and the technique of military discipline Frederick William constructed a primitive kind of totalitarian state in which everything was subordinated to the goal of military efficiency. The civilian existed to pay the taxes, and the taxes were imposed to pay the soldiers: the more taxes the more soldiers, and the more soldiers the more taxes. The state as a civil society could hardly be said to exist. It was little more than a haphazard collection of scattered territories which had no bond of unity except the Prussian government and the Prussian army. It was not until 1807 that the name of Prussia was used officially to designate the whole state. Yet even the army was not really a national one. It consisted in almost equal proportions of foreign mercenaries and conscript peasants welded together by the iron rod of Prussian discipline: a vast automatic fighting machine, the like of which could only be found in Russia, where its existence was largely due to the same Baltic colonial military caste which also formed the backbone of the Prussian army.

This was the army which in the hands of Frederick the Great raised Prussia to an equality with the great powers and more than doubled its territory and resources, though at the same time it increased its racial and national disunity by its Silesian and Polish acquisitions. The nineteenth century turned Prussia westwards and transformed the constitution of the Prussian state, but the Prussian tradition and the Prussian spirit never lost the character that had been indelibly imprinted by the inhuman genius of her two greatest kings: Frederick the Great and his father.

Now this Prussian tradition and the Prussian spirit were not only opposed to the tradition and spirit of Austria, which possessed the *de facto* and *de jure* leadership of the Reich in the eighteenth century. It was also opposed, and far more completely, to the spirit and tradition of the old Western German society which formed the first of the three Germanies already referred to. This Germany, as we have seen, was utterly lacking in political unity, and from the military point of view was so weak as to be incapable of self-defence against France or Prussia. It was a mosaic of miniature states—principalities, free cities, prince bishoprics and abbeys, and the estates of the imperial counts and knights who acknowledged no superior but the Emperor. Political conditions were not unlike those of Italy in the fifteenth century or those of Greece in the fourth century B.C., and as in those cases the lack of political unity and of social equality in no way prevented the development of a rich and active cultural life. Thus at the very time when Prussia was building up its rigid traditions of the absolute military state, Western Germany was creating the new humanist culture which finds expression in German classical literature. While in Prussia the army and the state were everything and the individual was nothing, in the humanist society of the west, culture transcended the state, and the enrichment of the individual personality was the only thing that counted.

It is true that a man like Goethe played a certain political role in the little state of Weimar, but he served his duke as Leonardo da Vinci served the Duke of Milan or Plato served the tyrant of Syracuse, in order to serve their own cultural ideals. The Potsdam of Frederick William I and the Weimar of Goethe are in fact the two opposite poles of the German development, and even the intelligence and the cosmopolitan culture of Frederick the Great were powerless to bridge the gap between them. It is true that men of Prussian origin, like Winckelman and Herder, played an important part in the development of German humanism, but they never regarded themselves as Prussians: indeed Winckelman once went so far as to say that he would rather be a Turkish eunuch than a Prussian! In the same way West Germans or Saxons like Lessing worked at Berlin and accepted pensions from the Prussian crown, as Leibnitz had done at an earlier period, but they did so in the same way that Greek philosophers and scholars served the Macedonians, without any idea of sacrificing their cultural freedom or their personal independence.

In this respect the old Prussia was not a totalitarian state, since it recognized its limitations: it was ready to use West German scholars as it used Scottish mercenaries or French men of letters, without attempting to make Prussians of them.

But the situation became entirely altered in the nineteenth century when Prussia had become a great power in Western Germany itself, and when there was a growing body of

opinion in both east and west which had come to regard
Prussia as the predestined champion of German national
unity.

For these changes, however, Prussia herself was not
primarily responsible. They were due, above all, to the
new forces awakened by the French Revolution throughout
Western Europe. The first effect of these changes was to
strengthen the influence of humanist culture and to increase
its cosmopolitan spirit, and even in Prussia itself it inspired
the two greatest Prussian representatives of the Enlightenment—Kant and Wilhelm von Humboldt—with a liberal
and individualist idealism which was the direct antithesis
of the old Prussian ideals of authority, obedience and
discipline.

Professor Gooch has shown in his *Germany and the
French Revolution* how universal was this wave of liberal
enthusiasm in the first years of the Revolution, and how
its effect was strongest on the minds of the very men who
became the leaders of the national awakening—like Fichte
and Görres. As in France the Jacobins had taken the lead
in a nationalist policy of military expansion and conquest,
so their disciples, the German Liberals, took the lead in
organizing the movement of national resistance to foreign
oppression. And since Prussia had been the chief victim
of French imperialism, it was to Prussia that the leaders of
the national awakening directed their propaganda and their
reforming efforts. Thus it was at Berlin that Fichte, the
ex-Jacobin, first formulated his ideal of totalitarian nationalism—the ideal of a new state which would embody the
total energies of the whole community—a *Kultur-Staat*
which would use the school and the university no less than
the army and the civil service as the instrument of a
common unitary purpose. Yet Fichte was not himself a
Prussian, and the same is true, as I have said, of most of

the other leaders in the national resistance. Stein, the reformer of the Prussian state, was a Rhinelander; Scharnhorst, the reformer of the Prussian army, was a Hanoverian. Neither of them was primarily concerned with Prussia. They were equally ready to accept Austrian or even English leadership, so long as this work to which they had dedicated themselves was done. The contrast between this new romantic nationalism and the old Prussian spirit is nowhere more sharply shown than in the canny, sceptical comments of Frederick William III on Scharnhorst's lyrical appeals for leadership, *"Gut als Poesie"*, and in Scharnhorst's reply, "The man who deals only with cold calculations becomes a sterile egotist. It is on poetry that the security of the throne depends".

The alliance between the German patriots and the Prussian state did not survive the War of Liberation. The dismissal of Stein and Gneisenau was followed by a reaction to the tradition of Prussian conservatism and led to an hostile and repressive policy towards popular nationalism. Nevertheless those decisive years had a profound influence on the development of both the elements which had participated in the struggle. During the first half of the nineteenth century the spirit of German humanism and romantic idealism had a broadening effect on Prussian culture which found full expression in the age of Frederick William IV and Radowitz; while in the west the nationalist ideology which had been created by the War of Liberation transformed the non-political humanist culture of eighteenth-century Germany, and produced a revolutionary movement of democratic nationalism which found a relatively harmless expression in the activities of the students' unions (the *Burschenschaften*) and the noisy demonstrations at the Wartburg and Hambach in 1817 and 1832.

The gulf between the two Germanies still remained unbridged. There seemed to be no room for any spiritual or social synthesis between the austere, conservative Prussian ethos of men like Roon and Marwitz and the democratic radicalism and the anti-religious rationalism of the Young Germans and the Young Hegelians. Yet both elements contributed to the achievement of national unity, and the Liberal Revolution of 1848 was the first stage of the movement which ultimately culminated in the foundation by Bismarck of the Second Reich. The fact that it was Prussian conservatism and not West German liberalism which provided the solution was not so much due to its inherent strength as to the superior quality of its leadership. Both on the intellectual and the political plane, the dominant figures were representatives of the Prussian idea. In the intellectual sphere Prussia found its philosopher and teacher in Hegel, the greatest of all the West German converts to the Prussian idea, while in the sphere of politics she found a statesman of the first rank in Bismarck, whose ruthless and revolutionary will to power was always subordinated to his spirit of traditional loyalty to the Prussian crown and the Prussian state. Yet in spite of their greatness, neither of these men was great enough to provide a final solution to the German problem. Hegel's political philosophy, which I discuss more fully in a later chapter, was a double-edged weapon which was to prove more effective in the hands of the social revolutionaries than in those of his orthodox disciples, the conservative defenders of the Hegelian ideal of a Prusso-German *Rechtstaat.*

The failure of Bismarck is even easier to understand. For with all his greatness he never aspired to be more than a great Prussian. The reconciliation of the conflicting tendencies and tensions in Germany and in Europe also demanded what Hegel calls a "World-Historical" figure, one who stood above and apart from the social forces which he aspired to dominate. But Bismarck was no Alexander or Caesar but a simple Prussian squire whose spiritual integrity depended on his loyalty to the Prussian tradition and the Lutheran ethos. It was only within these limits that his Machiavellian statecraft and his ruthless exploitation of power were tolerable. In the wider field of European and even Central European order he was a revolutionary and a destroyer. Hence his solution of the German problem was a limited one which could only endure so long as the social tradition on which it depended continued to survive. The Second Reich was unstable and impermanent, because it was based on the alliance between an unlimited German nationalism and the limited conservative tradition of the Prussian monarchy and the Prussian army, a solution which was essentially one-sided, since it left no room for some of the most deep-rooted elements in German culture.

What was left out? First, and above all, Austria. The exclusion of Austria did not mean merely the exclusion from Germany of the German population of the Austro-Hungarian monarchy; it meant the loss of one of the three Germanies, and with it the tradition of the old Reich of which Austria was the heir and the representative. For four centuries Austria had held the sceptre and had possessed a supernational hegemony and prestige that made her the centre of the European state system. This international position made Austria the natural mediator between Germany and the rest of Europe. She possessed links with the Low Countries in the west, with Italy in the south and with Hungary and the Balkans in the east, while her leadership of the Germanic Confederation linked her with the non-Austrian German states of the west and the north. Nowhere was there a rigid national and racial frontier which separated Austria from the rest of Germany or Germany from the rest of Europe.

But the severance of the bond between Austria and Germany in 1866 changed all this. The self-assertion of German nationalism in the Second Reich stimulated the forces of nationalism everywhere in Europe, and most of all among the subject nationalities of the Hapsburg Empire. The latter had now become a purely Danubian power which could only survive by identifying itself with the interest of the subject nationalities and giving them an equal share in the constitutional government of the Empire. But the more the government inclined towards this federalist solution, the more it aroused the dormant nationalism of its German subjects. It was this Austro-German and Bohemian-German opposition to the supernational tradition of the Hapsburg monarchy which, during the later nineteenth century, originated the Pan-German ideology, with its anti-Semitism, its anti-Catholicism and its cult of the pure Nordic race.

The acceptance of these anti-Christian, anti-humanist and anti-European ideas was in any case a retrograde step. But for Austria it was an act of spiritual suicide, since it meant the denial and destruction of all the spiritual values on which Austrian culture had been built. The Hapsburg monarchy had risen to greatness as the champion of a universal religious ideal and as the patron of an international Catholic culture. It had made use of men of the most diverse national origins—Italians and Spaniards, Magyars and Czechs, even French and Irish—in the service of this common cause. The later Austria which had been built on this Catholic foundation had developed its own type of humanist culture—the culture of the musicians, like Haydn and Mozart, and of the men of letters like Grillparzer and Adalbert Stifter—a humanism which was less self-conscious and less philosophical than that of West Germany but which was all the more deeply rooted in the social life of the Austrian people. Now all this was to be cast aside, and the common heritage of Baroque Austria and classical Vienna was torn to pieces between the rival fanaticisms of the Pan-Germans and the Pan-Slavs. Grillparzer, who remained loyal to the last to the old Austrian tradition, summed up the situation in 1848 in a prophetic sentence: "The path of modern culture leads from humanity through nationality to bestiality."

But if the exclusion of Austria from the new German unity destroyed Austria, its effects on Germany were also disastrous. The substitution of Prussia for Austria in the leadership of Germany meant the loss of just those qualities of political moderation and international responsibility which were precisely the qualities that were most necessary for a united Germany. Austria had acquired them painfully in the school of adversity, during the centuries in which she had had to navigate the unwieldy vessel of empire through the storms of war and revolution. But Prussia had risen to greatness by the exercise of just the opposite qualities—by the ruthless concentration of power on a single objective and by the courage of the gambler who is ready to risk everything on a decisive coup. When at last she had won the game and had acquired the power and riches of empire, she was unable to relax or to accept her responsibilities in a peaceful Europe. Her statesmen still looked at the world with the anxiety and uncertainty which their predecessors had shown when Prussia was a small and thinly peopled state fighting for existence among more powerful neighbours. In those days Prussia had achieved success by the ruthless efficiency of her military organization, which gave her an army out of all proportion to her population and wealth, and now that Prussia had become Germany, her statesmen applied the same technique to the immense resources of the new Empire. Strong as Germany was, she never felt herself to be strong enough, and the progressive increase of her military and naval power drove the rest of Europe down the fatal road of competitive re-armament which culminated in the First World War.

The catastrophe of 1918 threw Germany back into the melting pot. The work of Bismarck was undone. The German Empire and the Prussian monarchy were destroyed and the Prussian tradition, which was also the tradition of the German army, was discredited.

Nor could Germany look any longer for help and leadership to Prussia's historic rival, since the catastrophe of Austria was even more complete. Here the fall of the monarchy meant not merely the end of a tradition but the dissolution of the state. The great Empire which had held the gates of Europe against the Turks and had ruled the Danube for four centuries was swept away in a few weeks, and in its place there arose a group of small national states with no common bond save their hostility to Germany and their alliance with France.

In this situation the only course open for Germany was to return to the forgotten traditions of West German liberalism, which inspired the democratic constitution of the Weimar Republic. It was a solution that was doomed to failure from the beginning, since it was founded on failure and had to bear the burden of war guilt and reparations abroad and the responsibility for an unpopular peace and a disastrous economic situation at home. The appeal to the tradition of Weimar was merely a gesture of propaganda to cover the bankruptcy of the Second Reich. The Socialist Party, which was the leader of the new German democracy, found its spiritual home not at Weimar but at Berlin. Already in 1920 Oswald Spengler, who was one of the most influential writers of the Weimar period, maintained that there was a deep underlying affinity between Socialism and the Prussian tradition, and he demanded that the Socialists should discard their Marxism and the Conservatives their capitalism in order to form a common national-socialist front against the cosmopolitan liberal and Marxian influences which were undermining the German tradition. "Socialism," he writes, "spells Power." "*Macht, Macht und wieder Macht.*" We need hardness and Socialist supermen. The age of Goethe is past, what the world needs is a new Caesar, and the Prussian tradition is the only source in Europe from which such a new Caesar could arise.

Unfortunately the leader that Germany found was not a new Caesar but a new Catiline. Hitler himself was no Prussian. He had no real sympathy with the austere spirit of devotion to duty and the aristocratic conservatism of the old Prussian type. Nor was he a true Austrian, since he had a profound hatred for the Austrian state and the supernational ideals of the old Catholic Empire. But he possessed a genius for utilizing all the destructive and negative elements in the different German traditions—Austrian Pan-Germanism, Prussian militarism and *Machtpolitik,* South German political romanticism—each of which contributed its share to National Socialist ideology and the totalitarian party state. Thus Hitler succeeded at last in uniting the three Germanies and building a greater German Empire. But he did so at the expense of all that was best in both German and Austrian traditions. His victory led inevitably to the total war which has brought Germany, and Europe also, to a state of division and dissolution more complete than they have ever known, even after the Thirty Years' War.

Was Hitler the revenge of Austria for the wrong that was done to her by Bismark in 1866? Or was he the revenge of Prussia for her humiliation by the West and the German Democrats in 1918? The question is an unprofitable one.

All we can say is that there was once a Germany and there was once a Europe, and both of them have been destroyed.

But, little more than a hundred years ago, none of this was inevitable. Neither the Austria of Metternich nor the Prussia of Frederick William IV nor the Western Germany of the Frankfurt Liberals can be held responsible for the catastrophe. With all its faults the old Germanic Confederation still contained the elements of a solution which should take account of the complexity of the German problem and of the part which Germany might play in the evolution of international European order. Even Metternich, in spite of his political realism and his distrust of any kind of liberal idealism, was nevertheless the most European-minded of German statesmen and always sought to make the Germanic Confederation the keystone of European unity and the guarantee of European peace. Neither he nor his Prussian rivals in the leadership of Germany, nor the Liberal opponents of them both, were prepared to sacrifice the cause of Europe and the unity of Central Europe to a one-sided solution imposed by violence.

The fatal step was taken only when Bismarck decided to abandon the way of conciliation and to achieve national unity under Prussian leadership by the way of blood and iron. And it was the success of his Machiavellian statecraft and his ruthless use of military force which did more than anything else to change the current of public opinion in Germany and to popularize that worship of power and contempt for international morality which have had such a demoralizing effect on the German mind during the last eighty years. No doubt nothing could have been further from Bismarck's intention than the destruction of the moral character and authority of the German state. He saw himself as "God's soldier", and as an upholder of the Lutheran ideal of a Christian state. But, as his life-long opponent

Constantin Frantz pointed out, it is impossible, in the long run, for a state to represent the ideals of divine right and moral order in its internal relations, while it conducts its external relations by methods of organized piracy.

Although Frantz was himself a Prussian, he always maintained that the new Reich was merely a provisional system which could not endure because it was contrary to the natural doctrine of the state and to the interests of Europe as a society of Christian states. He believed that the true solution of the German problem was inseparable from that of the European problem and that both alike could only be found in a new system of federal organization. The attempt to transform Germany into a great centralized national state which was also a military empire was not only a danger to European peace, it was also contrary to the deep-rooted political traditions of the German people, which had always been based more than those of any other European people on the federal principle. Here he was thinking not so much of the modern Germanic Confederation, which was admittedly an artificial and inorganic structure, but of the older tradition of the Empire, which was based, on the one hand, on the principle of regional or territorial autonomy, and on the other, on the conception of a universal Christian society of which the Empire was the historic representative.

Even Bismarck's temporary and one-sided solution of the German and Central European problems would have been impossible without the existence of Austria and the alliance of the German Empire with the Dual Monarchy. Yet the very existence of the latter was irreconcilable with the principle of nationalism which was embodied in the Second Reich and which continued to act as a dissolvent force on the Hapsburg Empire, alike by the attraction it exerted on the German element in Austria and Bohemia and by the repulsion it provoked among the subject nationalities. When this contradiction was finally resolved by the dissolution of the Hapsburg Empire, when a united German nationalism was left face to face with the divided non-German nationalisms of the Succession states, the stage was set for the final tragedy which has involved Germany and the other Central European peoples in a common destruction.

At the present time Constantin Frantz's ideal of a great Central European federation which would unite Germans and Slavs in peaceful co-operation for supernational ends seems more remote than ever before. On the other hand, the wider idea of European federation has now become an urgent political question, and Germany—or at any rate Western Germany—occupies a key position in any solution that may be attempted. It is, however, difficult to suppose that the existing division of Europe can be a permanent one. Nevertheless the restoration of German unity can only be achieved either by the incorporation of the whole of Central Europe in a Western European federation or by the absorption of Western Germany, and Western Europe also, in a Communist world empire.

In either case there is no longer any room for a German empire of the Bismarckian type: indeed it already seems as though the age of the nation state has past and even a nation as powerful as Germany cannot survive unless it forms part of some wider unity.

CHAPTER V

Eastern Europe and Russia

IN the past, the European society of nations extended far beyond the limits of what is generally known as Western Europe. It included a number of kingdoms and nationalities which shared the intellectual and religious traditions of the West and made their contribution to the common stock of European culture. The political situation of these countries has been precarious for centuries, ever since the Turkish conquest of the Balkans and the rise of the military empires of Russia and Prussia, but their cultural community with Western Europe survived. It was not until the Second World War that this community was threatened, and it is the cultural separation of Eastern Europe from the West which is the most disastrous feature of the postwar world. For the new system of intercontinental power blocs cuts Europe asunder like a knife—and not Europe alone, for the division runs through the middle of Germany and Austria, so that Eastern Germany belongs to the same political bloc as North China, and Western Germany goes with North America, Australia and Japan.

Now in theory this division follows the lines of political ideology and party allegiance. The peoples and fragments of peoples east of the line are supposed to be convinced adherents of Communism, while those to the west accept the principles of constitutional democracy. In reality, however, it is essentially a matter of political and military power. It is a military frontier between two empires, or between an empire and the states and territories that remain independent of it.

A military frontier of this kind does not necessarily correspond to a line of division between different forms of culture:
indeed, it seldom does so. But in this case there is no doubt
that behind the conflict in power politics there is a deeper
ideological conflict between rival systems, and this ideological conflict tends to make the older cultural divergences
between Eastern and Western Europe serve its purposes. In
the past these divergences did not prevent the existence of
a common European culture and a considerable amount of
social and intellectual intercourse. But under the new
political conditions cultural relations are becoming increasingly difficult, so that we are faced with the danger of the
two rival power systems becoming two hostile spiritual
worlds with no bridge between them.

Hence it is our duty as Europeans to do all in our power
to understand what is happening in Eastern Europe and not
to accept the crude, oversimplified versions of history which
are so characteristic of the modern political ideologies. Unfortunately this is by no means easy for us in this country.
Few of us know Eastern Europe, fewer still can read or
speak its many languages, and still fewer are those who
have any wide knowledge of its history and its cultural and
religious traditions.

We have always been well aware of the importance of
Russia, and we know something of the inner history of
Russian culture owing to the riches of nineteenth- and early
twentieth-century Russian literature which has been so
widely translated. But between Russia and Germany and
Turkey there are nearly a dozen European peoples of whom
we know hardly anything, and whose whole history has
been left out of the ordinary Western education.

Consequently, when in 1917 the new Russia suddenly
forced itself on the attention of the Western world, the mind
of the English-speaking public was virgin soil prepared to

receive any seed that was sown in it. Public opinion veered between the naïve anti-Bolshevism of the post-1917 period and the equally naïve acceptance of Communist propaganda in the later 'thirties and the war years. Although the period between the wars saw the re-emergence of the suppressed nationalities of Eastern Europe, the only one of them which attracted much public attention was Czechoslovakia, thanks to the leadership of President Masaryk, whose ideas had so much in common with Western Liberalism. Throughout the whole time our main attention was focused on Russia, and we never made full use of our opportunities during this period to become acquainted with the history and culture of the other states of Eastern Europe, which have been traditionally a part of Catholic Europe and which have had far more in common with the West than Russia herself.

I do not wish to minimize the importance of Russia, for it is Russia, as we saw in the third chapter, that has dominated the whole development of events in Eastern Europe, and now threatens to dominate the world.

But it is essential that we should not simplify this development by identifying Eastern Europe with Russia and assuming that Russia is typical of Eastern Europe as a whole. It is this tendency that has led us to ignore or underestimate the importance of the independent elements in the East. It is here that our general ignorance of Eastern European history has been so misleading. The average Englishman knows nothing of the great age of free Eastern Europe. He does not realize that at the close of the Middle Ages, Poland and Hungary were great kingdoms which formed an integral part of Christendom and were by no means backward in culture as compared with the other states of Central and Northern Europe. Down to the sixteenth century Eastern Europe shared in the common cultural and religious life of Western Christendom; and the union of Poland with

Lithuania from the fourteenth century onward pushed the frontiers of this international society far out into what we regard as Russia—beyond the Dvina and the Dnieper and right down to the Black Sea. In those days Hungary, Poland and Bohemia were constitutional monarchies which possessed an active political life more like that of England or Aragon than that of the East, and in the same way their culture was influenced by the universities of Western Europe and by the new ideas of the Italian Renaissance. During these centuries Eastern and Northern Russia had passed completely out of the orbit of European civilization. To the Westerner in that age Russia meant Lithuania or Polish Russia—i.e. White Russia and Galicia and the Ukraine. Muscovite Russia, which was the ancestor of the modern Russian state, lay beyond the ken of the West in the mysterious world of Tartary—the lands of the Great Khan and the Golden Horde, which came into contact with Europe only on its southern flank through the Italian trading colonies of the Crimea and the Sea of Azov. And so when the first Western travellers and ambassadors visited Moscow at the end of the fifteenth and in the early sixteenth century they were like explorers who had discovered an unknown land.

This rediscovery of Russia came at a moment when the development of the other peoples of Eastern Europe was checked by the new advance of Islam, which severed the Christian nations of the Balkans from the rest of Christendom for five centuries. In 1453 Constantinople became the capital of the Ottoman empire. In 1526 Hungary suffered a catastrophic defeat and Buda became a Turkish Pashalik for 150 years. The mediaeval pattern of independent national kingdoms in South-Eastern Europe was replaced by two great military empires—the Ottoman power on the Bosphorus and the Hapsburg Empire on the Middle Danube.

Now the latter was a dynasty rather than a state—a dynasty whose possessions were scattered all over Europe, and were united only by loyalty to the Emperor and to the Church. Thus it was essentially international in character and, as we have seen, recruited its servants from every part of Catholic Europe in somewhat the same way as the Turks relied on Albanian and Greek viziers and recruited their army from the levy of Christian youths who formed the famous picked corps of Janissaries.

Thus among the mediaeval kingdoms of Eastern Europe Poland alone survived, and even for a time advanced in power and prosperity. During the sixteenth century, and the first decades of the seventeenth, Poland seemed destined to become the great power of Eastern Europe. By the union of the Polish and Lithuanian states at the Congress of Lublin in 1569, and the Union of the Churches at the Council of Brest in 1594, the Polish Republic acquired its definitive form as a constitutional elective monarchy of many races and religions which included the whole of Eastern Europe from the Turkish frontiers to those of the Hapsburg Empire, and to the remote frontiers of the Muscovite Empire in the far north. Had this experiment in federal constitutionalism proved successful, it would have changed the course of European history, since it represented a tradition that was diametrically opposed to that of the new military empires. Unfortunately the mediaeval tradition of constitutional government, which subjected the executive power to rigorous control, was ill-equipped for a struggle with the unfettered power of a military absolutism, and in the same way a system which favoured religious toleration was at a disadvantage in the age of the Thirty Years War when the rest of Europe was divided into two religious camps. But in spite of all this Poland might have survived had it not been for the tendency of successive Polish governments to embark on ambitious imperialist schemes with inadequate military and economic resources. It was, perhaps, inevitable that Poland should have taken advantage of the state of anarchy which followed the period of Ivan the Terrible to intervene in Russian affairs, and to extend the Union of Lublin by a union between Poland and Russia. But the fact that this scheme came so near to success in 1610–12 was responsible for a great revival of Russian national and religious patriotism, and this was followed by a similar reaction among the Orthodox population within Polish territory which culminated in the great Cossack revolt of 1648 that swept over the Ukraine like a deluge and endangered the very existence of the Polish Republic.

Poland never recovered from this disaster, which marks the turning point in Eastern European history. For though the Cossack revolt was a genuinely popular and even democratic movement which was inspired by the freedom of the steppes and aimed at an independent Ukrainian state, it actually resulted in the ruin of both the Ukraine and Poland to the benefit of Moscow. Slowly and irresistibly the Muscovite power advanced westward into Europe, and at the same time the influence of Western civilization began slowly and irresistibly to penetrate into Russia. This was a movement which resembled the penetration of Western culture into China and Japan in the seventeenth century. As J. B. Bury wrote, "The process was not an internal development, but rather like the laying of a mine which did not outwardly affect the land till Peter the Great had the courage to explode it." With tremendous hammer-blows of sword and axe and pick Peter cast the archaic oriental life of ancient Muscovy into the new mould of Western absolutism which found its centre and embodiment in the new Baltic capital built by forced labour in the swamps of the Neva.

And this revolution was carried out in the course of the Great Northern War, which lasted for twenty-one years from 1700–1721 and strained the resources of the new state to the uttermost limit of endurance. Out of this crucible of intense effort and suffering there emerged the new European Russia, which resembled neither the old Holy Russia of Muscovite tradition, nor the old Eastern European kingdoms of the Polish and Hungarian type. Although to Western eyes it still seemed a backward and barbarous power, it was in reality the first of the Enlightened Monarchies of the eighteenth century, since Peter the Great was a far more drastic innovator and a far more disinterested servant of the idea of the State than Louis XIV or Charles X of Sweden, or Frederick William of Prussia. It was he who launched not only Russia but the whole of Eastern Europe on a new path which had profound effects on the future development of the European state system.

For in modern times, in contrast to the Middle Ages, Eastern and Western Europe have followed divergent paths; and it is this divergence that has been one of the root causes of the catastrophic events of the present century. During the Middle Ages, Eastern Europe had followed a very similar line of development to that of the West. Latin Christendom had enlarged its boundaries to the east and north, bringing with it the same faith and culture, and the same education and law. In both regions the typical form of state was a national monarchy limited by the system of representative estates and corporate rights and privileges. In both the relations of Church and State were similar, and their religious and cultural institutions, such as the religious orders and the universities, were the same, though they were stronger and more numerous in the West.

In the eighteenth and nineteenth centuries religious unity

had been lost in both areas, but in the West the political tradition of the national monarchical state was still maintained, whereas the whole of Eastern Europe was now divided between four great military empires—Turkey, Russia, Austria and Prussia, which were superimposed on a number of subject peoples. The mass of the peasant population had, in many cases, sunk to a state of personal servitude lower than that which they had known in the Middle Ages. On the other hand, the rulers, except in Turkey, were in close contact with Western Europe, and were often themselves of Western origin, like Catherine the Great. They imitated Western fashions and manners, surrounded themselves with Western courts and ruled through Western ministers and generals.

The eighteenth century was the great age of Irish and Scottish soldiers of fortune—Patrick Gordon and Marshal Keith[1] and Peter Lacey in Russia, or Loudon and Browne[2] in Austria. It is typical of this cosmopolitan period that the reorganization of Southern Russia and the planning of Odessa was the work of the Duke of Richelieu, who was afterwards Prime Minister of France.

There has never been a system of government more detached from its roots in religion and nationality than that of the four Eastern European powers in the eighteenth century. It is true that each of them had its own official religion and its religious policy, but religion was habitually regarded as an instrument of government. Even in Catholic Austria, Joseph II regarded the clergy as salaried state officials whose business it was to co-operate with the police in the service of the state. The idea that religion was an independent

[1] J. E. F. Keith, brother of the tenth Earl Marischal, served in the Spanish army, commander of the Russian armies in the Turkish and Swedish wars, field marshal under Frederick the Great, and Governor of Berlin. Killed at Hochkirch, 1750.
[2] Ulysses, Count von Browne, 1705–1759, to be distinguished from George, Count Browne, 1698–1792, who was in the Russian service.

spiritual power to which even kings must bow seemed preposterous or out of date.

Never, in fact, has the game of power politics been played with more cool unscrupulousness and virtuosity than by those enlightened despotisms. As Frederick the Great wrote to his minister on the eve of the War of the Austrian Succession: "The question of *Right* is the affair of the ministries: it is *your* affair. Go ahead with it, for the orders to the troops have been given" (November 1740).

And it is remarkable that while the general level of culture was lower in the East than in the West, the ablest and most successful of the enlightened despots of the eighteenth century were to be found not in the West, but in Eastern Europe. Rulers like Peter I and Catherine II in Russia, Frederick the Great in Prussia and Joseph II in Austria, were the creators of a new state system which endured until 1914, and has left its mark even on the Europe that we know. It was characteristic of this order that, though the great powers were engaged in a constant diplomatic and military struggle, all of them, with the exception of Turkey, were animated by the same ideas and shared a common type of court culture, the international character of which is to be seen in the palaces and public buildings of Petersburg and Berlin and Vienna.

The same community of type is to be seen in their military organization. In this sphere they were pioneers and their transformation of military technique is hardly less important for modern history than the Western transformation of technique in industry. For as Professor K. Mannheim has pointed out,[1] the military organization of the absolutist states is the first great institution for the artificial production of uniform mass behaviour, and consequently it is one of the fundamental conditions of the modern totalitarian state.

[1] K. Mannheim, *Man and Society*, p. 255 (1940).

The problem these states had to solve was how to create an absolutely reliable military machine out of forced levies of illiterate peasant-serfs, whose whole interest was centred in their farm and their village and their parish church, and who often belonged to a different nationality and language-group from their rulers. The problem was most difficult for Russia, for its conscript armies had to be trained often by foreign mercenaries and always in foreign methods of drill and warfare, so that they should be capable of facing the national and professional armies of the West, above all that of Sweden, which united the *esprit de corps* of the professional soldier with a strong sense of nationality and a spirit of patriotic duty. At the cost of superhuman efforts and a complete disregard for human life and liberty, Peter the Great succeeded, and his achievements were so impressive that the Western states, in spite of their sense of cultural superiority, became his pupils and imitators.

The result of this achievement for Eastern Europe itself was nothing less than a profound change in spiritual values. The new army was the creator of the new state, and it took the place of the Church as the dynamic element in Eastern European society. Hitherto even in the West the rationalized planning of the statesmen and officials had affected only the upper surface of society, and the life of the peasant and the local village community had continued to follow its traditional way of life. But men like Peter the Great and Frederick the Great took hold of the whole social system and made it the instrument of their ruthless political will and intelligence.

And this was the more far-reaching in its effects because it was not yet limited by the national consciousness which had become so strong in the West. Throughout Eastern Europe the imperialism of the great powers produced an extraordinary intermixture of national minorities which were redistributed and shifted about according to the will of the rulers. How striking this difference was from what was known in the West may be seen in the following passage from a Scottish diplomat, Robert Murray Keith, whose business took him through the frontier territories of Hungary and Turkey at the end of the eighteenth century.

"One very strange thing," he writes, "is remarked by every traveller through the Banat. The villages are large, though distant, and we meet by turns Wallachian, German, Schlavonian and *French,* nay even *Italian* villages: the inhabitants of which have different languages, religions, manners, features and modes of garment; having no other intercourse with one another than that of mere necessity, and *never intermarrying.* A dash of the Gipsy nation and a sprinkling of Jews are met with everywhere, and the whole furnishes a grotesque and singular variety."[1]

These conditions also obtained in the new lands of Southern Russia, which were colonized in the later eighteenth and early nineteenth century, and on the frontiers of Russia and the Polish Lithuanian state, where they were of long standing. Indeed in many parts of Eastern Europe the intermingling of races tended to produce a sort of régime of fixed castes, so that the different social functions were performed by different peoples; a Magyar, Polish or Russian governing class of landlords, Rumanian, Slovak or White Russian peasant serfs, German townspeople and artisans, and Jewish pedlars and agents.

And the effect of this combination of local intermixture and social segregation and specialization was to increase the gulf between the life of the peasant community and the sophisticated cosmopolitan culture of the courts and the

[1] *Memoirs and Correspondence of Sir Robert Murray Keith,* II. 309 (1844).

capitals. This was most striking in Russia, where the small class which had received Western education regarded itself as a European colony among barbarians. And this cleavage between the French-speaking, German-trained ruling class and the servile masses was the more unfortunate because it replaced the natural and healthy process of cultural contact between the neighbouring peoples of Eastern Europe through which Polish culture had reached Russia through the Ukraine and Lithuania in the seventeenth century.

Thus the rise of the new absolute state not only meant a change in the spiritual balance of power and the increasing predominance of the new powers of Russia and Prussia: it also meant that religion had everywhere become subordinated to the state and occupied both a smaller and a lower place in social life. In fact the attitude of the enlightened despotisms towards the religion of their subjects was not unlike that of the Western colonial powers towards the religion and culture of oriental peoples.

Even the Austrian Empire, which was the one remaining Catholic power in Eastern Europe, was not exempt from this change, since the reforms of Joseph II went far to make the Church in the Austrian dominions an instrument of the bureaucratic state, and the one great independent organ of Catholic culture in the Counter-Reformation period, the Society of Jesus, had already been destroyed by the action of the Catholic powers themselves.

The case of Prussia is more complex. On the one hand, it is the most perfect example of the new type of rationalized military absolutism—the most completely military in origin and the most efficient in its soulless bureaucratic despotism. And it had the good or evil fortune to be ruled by two perfect examples of their respective types—Frederick William I, the crowned sergeant-major, and Frederick the Great, the most enlightened of the enlightened despots. Yet at the same time Prussia even in the eighteenth century had a dual character. She faced westward as well as eastward, and it was through her expansion to the West, and her eventual alliance with Western German nationalism, that she ultimately reached her full stature as a great European power.

This dual development was of epoch-making importance for both Eastern and Western Europe. In the East, Prussia was the representative of Western efficiency and Western science; while to the West she revealed new possibilities of power, not only in war and military organization, but in the idea of the state itself as the supreme principle of social and economic organization. It is no accident that Karl Marx was a Prussian, though he was a Prussian of the West. And the impatient contempt he shows for the backwardness and barbarism of the East, and for the individualism and indiscipline of the West, is not unlike that of the traditional type of Prussian officer or bureaucrat.

It was the rise of Prussia which completed the modern state-system of Eastern Europe. While Western Europe was undergoing a far-reaching process of political change, and bourgeois liberalism and constitutionalism were everywhere supreme, Eastern Europe was immobilized under the firm grip of the three great military powers whose mutual cooperation remained the cornerstone of the Eastern European system from the days of Metternich to those of Bismarck, in spite of the fact that Germany itself was the scene of intense rivalry and conflict between Austria and Prussia.

However much the three Empires might disagree, they remained tied together by their common responsibility, and their common share in the partitions of Poland in 1772, 1793, and 1795. This was the keystone of the imperialist order in Eastern Europe, and the Three Partitions determined the character of the age and the society in Eastern Europe, in the same way as the English, the American and the French

Revolutions determined the character of the liberal order and the bourgeois society in the West.

It is true that these Western movements were not without their influence in the East. They reawakened the demand for freedom and the cult of national traditions, not only in Poland, but also in Hungary, Bohemia and the Balkans. This renaissance of the old national traditions was everywhere accompanied and strengthened by a religious revival, which was also of Western origin, and which challenged the control of religion and culture by the state. In Germany the great struggle between the Church and Bismarck was already foreshadowed by the conflict which united the Catholics of the Rhineland and the Polish provinces in their resistance to the Prussian government during the 'thirties. In Austria the Church began to react against the tradition of Josephinism. In Poland the Catholic Church kept alive the traditions of Polish culture against both German and Russian pressure, while even in Russia itself the Slavophils, in spite of their exaggerated nationalism, made a real effort to recover the spiritual independence of the Orthodox Church and to resist the secularization of Russian society by a Westernized and German-educated bureaucracy. The great achievements of Russian literature in this age, from the time of Gogol onwards, owes much to values of the old Christian tradition and to the stimulus of the conflict between Western secular enlightenment and Christian traditionalism: though we must not forget the existence and the influence of Western religion, whether Catholic, as with Chadaaev and Soloviev, or Protestant, as with Tolstoi and many less well-known but more orthodox thinkers.[1]

But the intellectual and spiritual revival of Eastern Europe which produced such brilliant results in the inner world of

[1] As early as the eighteenth century St. Tychon of Zadonsk translated or adapted a work by the seventeenth-century Bishop of Norwich, Joseph Hall.

literature and ideas was denied any outlet in the world of political and social action by the iron hand of Tsarist autocracy which was never heavier or more harsh than during the reign of Nicholas I (1825–55). Consequently the new forces in Russian society were driven underground and forced to seek expression in subterranean revolutionary channels. Never was the influence of the West stronger than in these years, but since there was no room in Russia for Western Liberalism of the parliamentary type, it was the most revolutionary elements in Western thought which had the deepest influence on the Russian mind. All through the nineteenth century this underground movement of resistance continued to develop, fed by the propaganda of political exiles like Herzen, Bakunin and Tkachev, and occasionally exploding in outbursts of terrorist activity. Under these conditions "Western" ideas no longer acted as a bridge between Russia and the rest of Europe, but became an explosive force which widened the gap between them. Thus when the Tsarist Empire finally collapsed as a result of the First World War, this tradition of uncompromising revolutionary extremism proved too strong for the liberal democratic elements represented by the Provisional Government, and its victory divided Russia from the West more completely than Tsarism had ever done.

It was the hope of Western idealists like President Wilson and idealists in Eastern Europe like President Masaryk that the new order which followed the fall of the three military empires would follow the same pattern of liberal constitutional national democracy as existed in the West, and that East and West would co-operate in the creation of a democratic world order which would find its organ in the League of Nations.

Actually they proved wrong. The tradition of absolutism was stronger than they realized, and out of the ruin of the

old empires there arose the far more formidable and inhuman power of the totalitarian state.

There is no need to insist on the momentous character of
this development. It is the one point on which there is no
difference of opinion between totalitarians and anti-totali-
tarians. Both sides agree that it marks a complete break
alike with the existing democratic or capitalist order in
Western Europe, and also with the old Christian culture
of Eastern Europe, whether Catholic or Orthodox. Everything else, however, is a matter of controversy. For though
it can hardly be denied that the new type of state involves
dictatorship, the identification of state and party, and the
institution of a more rigorous form of police control than
anything known hitherto, these are features which the Communist state shares with National Socialism, and it is well
known that Communists and Nazis have both repudiated the
idea of their fundamental community of type, which seems
obvious to the outside observer.

But it is when we come to the fundamental question of
origins and ends that the conflict of opinion becomes most
acute. The Communist is bound by his creed to interpret
the revolution in orthodox Marxian terms as the inevitable
product of the class conflicts of capitalist society; so that it
belongs to Western Europe and America as much, or even
more, than it does to the East, because it was in the West
that bourgeois capitalism developed first and transformed
society most completely. But during the last century Western
society has been steadily finding its own solutions to its
problems, which were not those that Marx predicted. The
Communist revolution came in the East as a result of a
particular Eastern European development which Karl Marx
had never envisaged.

The totalitarian state is not a transitional stage in the
evolution of the Marxian ideal of a classless society. It is

a monstrous hybrid born from the unnatural union of the Western revolutionary tradition with the Eastern tradition of the military police state. The Marxian dialectic of class war may be the source of its ideology and its propaganda, but the real sources of its political power are to be found in the techniques of absolute bureaucratic government and military mass control that were developed by the three great Empires of Eastern Europe during the last two or three centuries.

This may seem a paradox, but we cannot ignore the fact that Eastern European society had been subjected to a severe and intensive process of mass conditioning which could not fail to leave its mark on men's thought and behaviour. While the Western people were developing the new industrial techniques and the new capitalist order of trade and finance, the Eastern peoples were being drilled in quite a different school by the professional soldiers and police officers of the giant Eastern monarchies. These powers had gone so far to transform the social pattern, and held such a large place in Eastern European life, that their sudden collapse created a void which was felt even by those who had suffered from their power and had longed for their downfall. It was like the case of the man in the parable out of whom an evil spirit had been expelled, and who remained an empty house, swept and garnished, until he was invaded by seven other devils stronger than the first. There was a change of personnel and a change of class, but the old techniques of autocracy and mass power were reinforced and not diminished.

In Russia the autocracy left its old half-way house in Peter the Great's new capital and went back to Moscow and the Kremlin. This retreat, together with the collapse of the other two Empires, made it possible for the old peoples of Eastern Europe to re-emerge and to regain their long-lost national sovereignty. But this was only a momentary episode.

The political renaissance of the Eastern European states was cut short by the rise of a second totalitarian state—the German Third Reich.

This was another example of the same process as that which had transformed the Tsarist autocracy into the Communist dictatorship. The Weimar Republic, as its name suggests, represented the anti-militarist, anti-Prussian, Western, liberal, democratic elements in the German tradition. But Hitler and the National Socialist movement deliberately turned their backs on the West, and revived the tradition of the Prussian army and the Prussian state, together with the ideal of imperial expansion in Eastern Europe. They did in fact recreate the old militarist power-state in a new modernized, streamlined, mechanized form. And the constitutionalist national states of Eastern Europe were unable to oppose the converging pressure of these two reorganized mass powers. History has never repeated itself more dramatically than when Hitler and Stalin followed in the footsteps of Frederick and Catherine the Great and concluded the agreement for the partition of Poland which led to the World War, and thus ultimately to the partition of Germany itself and to the division of Europe.

For Eastern Europe the results of this division have been revolutionary in every sense of the word. The old relations of these countries with Central and Western Europe which had moulded their history and culture for nearly a thousand years have been brought to an abrupt end, together with their short-lived political independence which they enjoyed between the two wars. To-day they have become satellites of the vast Soviet Empire which stretches from the Baltic to the Pacific, while their social and economic structure is being transformed in accordance with the Communist pattern. This revolution is not only a political and social one, it is also a revolution of culture. For the liquidation of the old ruling classes means the removal of those elements which were most Western in education and social contacts, and the substitution of a new Russian-trained governing class which is inspired by Russian ideology and is obedient to the commands of Moscow. Thus the whole of Eastern Europe has been lopped away from the trunk of Western culture and grafted into the new totalitarian organism which has grown up in Russia and Northern Asia during the last thirty years.

CHAPTER VI

Russia and Asia

R USSIA is not a country like the countries of Western Europe—a nation among the nations—it is a world apart which still remains a mystery to the average Westerner. There is no end to Russia—it is a land without frontiers, which stretches back endlessly in place and time. It is an open road into the heart of Asia. Along this road have come the great conquering peoples of the past—Huns and Avars, Khazas and Bulgars, Cumans and Mongols. They have founded their empires and passed away, but the Russian land remains.

For Russia did not come out of Asia. There is another road—a river road—through the East European forests from the Baltic to the Black Sea, and it was here that Russia was born in the borderland between the forest and the steppe, at a moment when the pressure from Asia was temporarily relaxed. It was a state of merchant warriors organized by Viking adventurers along the chain of trading posts and portages which connected Scandinavia with the Black Sea and the Byzantine Empire, the centre of Christian civilization from which Russia received its religion and the higher elements of its culture.

During the eleventh and twelfth centuries Kievan Russia enjoyed a short period of prosperity and culture. It was in contact with the Byzantine world through the Black Sea and with Northern and Western Europe through Novgorod and the Baltic, and it also advanced north-eastward to Vladimir and Suzdal and Rostov in the region of the Upper Volga.

If it could have survived, the whole history of Europe would have been profoundly altered, and Christendom as a whole might have attained an organic unity which it never actually achieved. But in the thirteenth century the pressure of the steppe was renewed suddenly and catastrophically by the Mongol invasions.

In six years, from 1236 to 1242, the Mongol armies swept across Eastern Europe in a whirlwind of destruction which levelled everything that stood in its path. When they withdrew, not on account of any European resistance but owing to the death of the Great Khan, they left behind them a vast devastated area that extended from the Volga to the Oder and the Adriatic. Poland and Hungary gradually recovered and took up the broken thread of their political existence. But the whole Russian land remained a subject province of the Mongol world empire.

Thus Kievan Russia came to an untimely end and the centre of Russian population and culture shifted to the region of the Upper Volga, where they absorbed and overlaid the older Finnish population which had once inhabited the whole forest region from the Baltic to the Urals. This was the Second Russia, the land of Muscovy which was lost to Europe for three centuries. It still remained faithful to the spiritual tradition of Byzantine and Kievan Russia, but politically and economically it became a part of Asia. From prehistoric times the Middle Volga had been a focus of culture, and throughout the early Middle Ages, from the eighth to the thirteenth century, the Moslem state of Bolgar at the junction of the Volga and the Kama was one of the main centres of commerce between Northern Europe and Central Asia. From the earliest times this trade route by the Volga and the Caspian to Central Europe had rivalled that of the Dnieper and the Black Sea to Constantinople, and had caused a very early Russian

colonization of the region between the Upper Volga and
the Oka.

Now in the thirteenth century the road to Constantinople
was closed by the Mongol conquest, while Western Russia
gradually became a part of the Lithuanian state. Meanwhile
the old Bulgarian centre on the Middle Volga had ceased
to exist, and its place was taken by the Tartar capital of
Sarai, near Stalingrad, whose ruler was the overlord of all
the Russian cities. It was as the agent and tax-gatherer of
the Tartar Tsar that the Prince of Moscow acquired his
supremacy, which he owed not to his military power but
to his diplomacy and subservience to the Tartar yoke.

During the next two centuries Russia went through a
period of suffering and humiliation which made a deep
impression on the national consciousness. It was not merely
that the country suffered from periodic Tartar raids and
devastations and from the enslavement of part of the population; even worse was the moral effect of the harsh struggle
for existence among the surviving Russian states, which led
them to denounce one another to their Tartar overlords and
to bribe the Tartar officials to destroy their weaker neighbours.

Under these conditions there was little inducement or
opportunity for cultural life, and it was only through the
work of the Orthodox Church that the tradition of Russian
culture was kept alive. The later Middle Ages saw a great
development of Russian monasticism. It was no longer a
predominantly urban movement, as in the Kievan period,
but a true *anachoresis*, a flight to the desert. The disciples
of St. Sergius of Radonezh and St. Cyril of Belozerk founded
their hermitages and desert monasteries in the depth of
the northern forests from the Upper Volga to the frozen
Arctic Sea, and these monastic settlements were gradually
followed by a movement of peasant colonization.

Thus this period of suffering and isolation between the thirteenth and the sixteenth century had a profound effect on Russian character and destiny. It forged the Russian people into a solid mass with immense powers of endurance and resistance, but completely devoid of the personal humanist culture which had been growing up in the West during the later Middle Ages. This tradition had also existed at Byzantium, but it was not part of the Byzantine heritage which Russia had received. The new Russia was a theocratic autocracy which regarded itself as the Third Rome, the successor of the Byzantine Empire, but which actually took the place of its old suzerain, the Tartar Empire of the Volga.

In the late fifteenth century, during the reign of Ivan III, the Muscovite state suddenly grew from a local principality on the Moskva and the Upper Volga to an imperial power which embraced the whole Russian land east of Poland and Lithuania, and at the same time its ruler was transformed from the chief amongst a number of semi-independent princes into "the Tsar and Autocrat of All Russia" who exercised a greater power over the lives and property of his subjects than any Byzantine Emperor. The first Western observers who visited Russia about this time were immediately impressed by the autocratic character of the Muscovite state. Herberstein, the ambassador of Maximilian to Vassili III (1505–33), declares that the Tsar was more absolutely supreme over his subjects than any other monarch in the world, and he quotes the common Russian saying, "The will of the Tsar is the will of God, and of the will of God the Tsar is the fulfiller".

When, in the sixteenth century, this new power at last emerged from its forests to conquer the Middle and Lower Volga and thus close the road from Asia, it changed the course of history far more fundamentally than by its slow and difficult progress towards the west. Without any spec-

tacular wars or victories it gradually spread irresistibly over
the whole of northern Asia from the Volga to the Pacific
—so that the breeding ground of the nations, the home of
the nomad peoples who had for thousands of years des-
cended in a destructive torrent on the settled civilizations
of the ancient and mediaeval worlds, was brought into
subjection to the peasant race of the northern forests.

The advance was much more rapid in the east than in
the south, since Russia had reached the Pacific by 1636
when the first port was established on the Sea of Okhotsk,
whereas it was not until 1792 that she finally established
herself on the northern coast of the Black Sea and in the
Crimea. But this expansion was not altogether the work of
Muscovite Russia. Both in the east and the south, as well
as south-westward in the Ukraine, the advance was led by
a very different element—the free Cossacks of the Steppes.
These Cossack communities had developed in the no-man's-
land between Muscovy and Tartary, and they had more in
common sociologically with the Tartar horsemen than with
the Russian peasant. It was the revolt of the Cossacks of
the Dnieper against Poland that led to the recovery of Kiev
and the Eastern Ukraine by Russia in the middle of the
seventeenth century and the decline of the Polish power.
But the Russian Cossacks of the Don and the Yaik often
proved as insubordinate to Moscow as those of the Dnieper
were to Poland, and it was with them that the great popular
insurrections of the seventeenth and eighteenth centuries
originated—the rising of Stenka Razin in 1670 and that
of Pugachev in 1773–75.

The lawless freedom of the Cossack communities was in
fact entirely irreconcilable with the dominant tendency in
the Russian state itself. For the same age which saw the
imperial expansion of Russia also saw the progressive decline
of the free elements in Russian society—the enslavement of

the peasants to the landowners, the absorption of the nobles in the official class, and the complete subordination of the officials to the autocratic power of the Tsar. The whole tendency of the Russian political system was in the direction of the autocracy, and this was by no means entirely due to the despotism of individual rulers, like Ivan the Terrible and Peter the Great, since it continued to develop consistently throughout the sixteenth and seventeenth centuries, apart from the temporary anarchy of the Time of the Troubles, from 1605 to 1613.

This is strikingly exemplified in the reign of Alexis Mikhailovitch, who was personally one of the gentlest and most humane men that ever occupied the Russian throne. Yet it was under his rule (1645–76) that the bloody and terrible persecution of the Old Believers took place, and the same spirit of inhuman severity marked the suppression of the Moscow riots of 1662 and the revolt of Stenka Razin in 1671.

The accounts of Russian conditions by both native and foreign observers which become numerous at this period all agree on the unlimited power of the Tsar and the intense severity with which it was exercised. Perhaps the most interesting of these observers is the Serbian priest, Yuri Krizhanitch, who came to Russia as a Catholic missionary in 1659 and became the earliest exponent of Pan-Slavist ideas. Although Krizhanitch fully realized the cultural backwardness of the Russian people and the need for a far-reaching programme of reform, he had unbounded faith in the future of Russia as the destined leader of the Slav peoples and in the possibility of achieving this destiny by governmental action. He looked to the Tsar both to undertake the work of internal reform and to achieve the liberation of the other Slav peoples from foreign rule, and he concludes: "Thou, O Tsar, dost hold in thine hands the miraculous rod of Moses, with which thou art able to work wonders in the government. For in thy hands, there is full autocracy."

Krizhanitch received little recognition from Alexis and left Russia, a disappointed man, in 1677. But he was a true prophet, since all that he had foreseen was realized and exceeded by "the miraculous rod of autocracy" as wielded by the son of Alexis, Peter the Great. In the course of a single generation Peter changed the course of Russian history, and his work has left an indelible impression on Russian culture. With all his faults, which were many and great, he was one of the greatest rulers that the world has seen. Without sparing himself or any one else, he drove his people relentlessly along the hard road to civilization. By sheer will-power and by thirty years of unremitting labour he triumphed over the dead weight of tradition, the inertia of the national character, the resistance of the aristocracy, the peasantry and the Church and the hostility of foreign powers, so that before he died the Russian state and society had been transformed from top to bottom.

But the very greatness of his achievement involved an element of weakness, since it owed everything to the autocratic will of a superman and had no organic relation to the older traditions of Russian culture. For the introduction of Western civilization into Russia and her entry into the European society of nations was not a spontaneous national awakening but the forcible imposition of an alien pattern of thought and behaviour which outraged the deeper feelings and prejudices of the people. Hence the divided state of the national consciousness which characterized the whole period from Peter the Great to Nicholas II. There was the world of St. Petersburg with its Western architecture, its Western culture and social life, its Western bureaucratic and military order, and there was the world of the people— peasants and merchants and clergy—which still had its roots deep in the Muscovite past. But these two worlds were continually interpenetrating one another. The influence of the bureaucracy was felt in the village and in the Church, while the more highly educated the ruling class became, the more sensitive it was to the existence of the popular underworld.

The brilliant flowering of Russian culture in the nineteenth century, above all in the sphere of literature, was a result of this process of interaction. It was the work of the educated classes, who had turned their faces to the West and fully shared in the intellectual life of European culture, but who at the same time felt a nostalgia for their native soil and its popular traditions and a sense of guilt for the enslavement of the peasantry which was the economic basis of Russian society. Some of them, like the Slavophils, believed that the work of Peter the Great had been a gigantic mistake and that the salvation of Russia was to be found in a return to the pre-Petrine traditions of Holy Russia. Others, who included the majority of the intelligentsia, believed that the process of Westernization had not gone far enough and that it should be completed by a revolutionary process of political and economic reform. But both parties agreed in their criticism of the existing régime, which was neither genuinely Russian nor Western European, and in their faith in the Russian people and its destiny.

For the Slavophils that destiny was to be found in the realization of the ideal of Christian society which had been lost by the rationalism and materialism of the West. To the Westernizers it was to be found in the spirit of Socialism or Communism which was in harmony with the needs of the expropriated and oppressed Russian people, whereas it ran counter to the development of modern bourgeois culture and the parliamentary institutions of the Western European state. The fundamental community of these two ideals is to be seen in the writings of the exiles, like Herzen and Bakunin, who did so much to indoctrinate the Russian intelligentsia with their ideas. For both of them were Socialist Slavophils who believed that the Russian peasant community preserved the germ of a true Socialist society which was lacking in the more sophisticated and individualistic culture of Western Europe.

In the same way there was a distinctively Russian spirit in the Nihilist movement, which contributed so much to the revolutionary movement in Russia during the second half of the nineteenth century. For its denial of cultural and moral values and its cult of violence and destruction was really directed against the alien values and the alien order that had been built up by Peter the Great and his successors, and it had something in common with the peasant Jacqueries and Cossack revolts which had been endemic in Russia since the seventeenth century. Indeed Bakunin himself was a kind of modern Pugachev whose lust for destruction found expression in ideological theorizing as well as in revolutionary action.

It was the great tragedy of modern Russia that the extremist tendencies in the Russian revolutionary movement came to a head at the same moment when the government and the ruling classes had accepted the need for reform and had actually carried out the fundamental measure of the abolition of serfdom. But the assassination of the Tsar Liberator in 1881 drove the government back on a policy of reaction and destroyed the hope of social reconciliation and peaceful reform. The old Nihilist and terrorist organizations were indeed successfully repressed, but their place was taken by the Russian Marxists, who eventually inherited the whole tradition of the revolutionary movement.

For though Marxism was a Western ideology, based on the philosophy of Hegel and Feuerbach and the history of

Western capitalism and of the Industrial Revolution, it was not without elements which had a special appeal to the Russian mind. In the first place, there was the authoritarian element which imposed a strict standard of dogmatic orthodoxy and demanded the complete subordination of the individual will to the party discipline. In the second place, there was the historical fatalism which insists on the irresistible and inevitable character of the process of social change which is leading to the Communist state.

And finally there was the Messianic spirit which regards the proletariat as destined to liberate humanity from its age-long servitude to the forces of economic exploitation and to create the new order of social justice.

It was the first of these elements that proved the most decisive in the personality and work of Lenin, through which the fusion between Marxian Communism and the Russian revolutionary tradition was finally achieved. Lenin was a born organizer with an intense will to power. It was he who forged the iron party discipline of the Bolshevik party and who transformed the Marxian theory of the dictatorship of the proletariat into the practical autocracy of a minority party based on revolutionary violence.

Consequently, when the Tsardom fell Lenin found little difficulty in defeating the liberal idealists, as represented by the Provisional Government, and in carrying out the total social revolution towards which the Russian revolutionary movement had so long aspired.

Not only the bureaucracy, but much older and deeper things were destroyed—the Tsardom, which was the common factor between the Muscovite and Petersburg periods, and the Orthodox Church, which had been the spiritual frame of Russian society from the beginning. On the ruins, amidst civil war and terror and famine, the foundations of yet another Russia were laid.

But though this new Russia was ruthlessly and totally planned according to the strict canons of scientific Marxian Socialism, it did not altogether eliminate the dualism that is inherent in the whole development of modern Russia. Looked at from one point of view it is the culmination of the Westernizing movement, the triumph of Western science, Western Socialism, and Western democracy. The Russian declarations of the Rights of Man, in their later amplification in the Constitution of 1936, actually went farther in the theoretic recognition of personal freedom than any of the Western democracies. They proclaimed freedom of religion, freedom of speech, universal suffrage, and the inviolability of the person and the domicile. But this was only one side of the picture—and a deceptive one at that. The Revolution turned back Russia from Petersburg to Moscow, from the classical façade of the Winter Palace to the exotic silhouette of the Kremlin. Its makers and rulers are men from the east—Lenin, a man of Tartar ancestry from the Volga steppes, and Stalin, a Georgian from the Caucasus. Finally, while it destroyed the class hierarchy of Tsarist Russia, and the exterior apparatus of the monarchy, the underlying reality of absolute power was maintained and even strengthened. Always the tendency has been that Russia is everything and the individual nothing, but never has it been so much so as in the Russia of the Soviets. Never before has the will of the government been so able to change the minds and direct the actions of every man and woman. From Leningrad to Vladivostock, the whole vast mass has been welded into a unity guided by a single brain and will.

Are we then to conclude that Communist Russia is simply a new Eurasian imperialism in the tradition of the Asiatic world empires of the past? Or is it a real attempt to assert the rights of the submerged and oppressed masses? This is the great question that has interested and divided Western opinion so deeply, but in order to answer it, it is necessary to remember that the totalitarianism of Russia is a Russian fact which cannot be fitted into the cadres of Western tradition and experience.

In the first place, we must remember how deeply the iron of slavery has bitten into the Russian soul. There has never been a time when slavery was not a dominant fact in Russian social experience. The very origins of Russia were bound up with the slave trade, and it was the great source of supply for the slave markets of Constantinople and the Volga. In the second period of Russian history, the people lived under the perpetual menace of the great Tartar slave raids which depopulated the southern provinces and which did not end till the eighteenth century. Lastly, the whole of the third period, from the seventeenth to the nineteenth centuries, was dominated by the institution of serfdom, which reduced the mass of the peasantry to a condition of personal slavery. A people that has endured such things cannot regard the state and the rights of man with the eyes of Western man. When we were developing an individualist, humanist, competitive society the Russian people was living in the dark, storing up its immense resources of patience and resentment—and at the same time immense powers of faith and hope. As one of Gorki's characters puts it:

"The people live by their dreams—they need to have strong imaginations to enable them to withstand the hardships of life, to resign themselves to their life; for it's the only life they are likely to know on this earth. . . . Life is not a blessing to them and will never be a blessing, but it will be for ever and ever an expectation, a hope that it will become a blessing. The people need a hero, a saint. . . . And the more remote, the more vague, the less accessible the hero, the more freedom for the imagination, the easier it is to live. There must be a 'once upon a time' about it—something of the fairy tale. Not a God in heaven, but here, on our dismal earth. Someone of great wisdom and monstrous power; someone who should be all-powerful, who would merely have to wish it and everybody would be happy. . . .

"So that to try to prove to the people that the Romanoffs are Germans is useless. It is all the same to them: they might be Mordovians[1] for all they care. I tell you I know the people! They do not need a democracy, they have no use for an English Parliament, they do not care for organized machinery of any kind—they want mystery. They need the power of a great unit, of a great entity, even though that entity be zero: they will fill the zero with their own imagination."[2]

If this is in any sense true, then it can hardly be denied that totalitarianism has a significance for Russia quite other than it can ever have for the West, for it is not an artificial construction imposed from outside on the free tradition of a political society, but something that has its roots within, in the Russian past and the Russian soul. It has come out of the non-political past, out of the night of serfdom and the anonymous existence of submerged masses and subject races.

It has, moreover, its spiritual counterpart in the Russian religious tradition, which always tended to identify the Russian people and even the Russian state with the Orthodox Church. Russia has always been a theocracy, a single

---

[1] The Mordvinians are one of the native Finno-Ugrian peoples of European Russia. Under the Soviets they formed one of the "Autonomous Republics" of the R.S.F.S.R., with their capital at Saransk, south of the Volga.

[2] "Breef the Dreamer," in *Fragments from My Diary*, pp. 213–14, Penguin Ed.

community which was both Church and State. In this it resembles the great "monolithic" civilizations of the ancient East—Egypt, Babylonia, China—rather than the dualist or pluralist civilization of the West. And thus the relation between Ideology, Party and State in the new Russia follows the same pattern as that of Orthodoxy, Church, and Empire in the old order, and the fact that the ideology of the Soviet régime is Western in origin does not prevent its being profoundly different in its social effects. It has often been noted that the Russian attitude to Communism is a thoroughly religious one and that materialism is accepted positively as a faith, rather than negatively as in the West, where it is rather the absence of faith. And this combination of a materialist creed with a religious attitude is not peculiar to Bolshevism, it is characteristic of the Russian revolutionary tradition, whose leaders were so often ascetics and saints of rationalism, like Dobrolyubov and Chernyshevsky.

In the same way, the new Russian state, in spite of its original will to be the state of the workers, remains an imperial and autocratic society, so that the work of Lenin and Stalin has more in common with that of Peter the Great than with any Western revolution.

The Communist régime has inherited many of the most odious features of the old autocracy—the secret police, the censorship, the internal passport system, the ruthless suppression of minority opinions and the "liquidation" of hostile classes and groups. Yet all these things run directly counter to the theoretical principles of the régime—as expressed, for example, in the Constitution—as well as the revolutionary tradition itself. For the whole revolutionary struggle in the century between the beginning of the Decembrist Movement and the victory of the Revolution was inspired by the determination to destroy these things and to right the wrongs of the oppressed and the exploited.

We see the nature of this contradiction most clearly in the character of Lenin himself. No man was more sincere in his devotion to the revolutionary ideal and to the cause of the people, but at the same time as a politician and a ruler he had a completely imperial attitude to power which recalls that of Peter the Great. But whereas Peter's work was weakened and disturbed by the German princelings and courtiers who succeeded him, Lenin found a successor who developed the imperial element in his policy and based it firmly and deliberately on its historic national foundation.

Whatever we may think of Russian Communism as a system of social democracy, there can be no question of its success as a system of organized power. Of all the world empires it is the most unitary and the most totalitarian. For its federalism and the wide constitutional rights accorded to the constituent national units does not prevent each and all of them being controlled entirely by a single will and a single purpose. And this is rendered possible by the revolutionary dictatorship exercised through the Communist Party in the U.S.S.R. as a whole, and in its constituent states. Russia, as Stalin himself has said, is not a nation: it is a union of nationalities, but the basis of this union is a single organization of absolute power—a party autonomy based on iron discipline and recognizing no restriction or limit.

But if the U.S.S.R is still an empire rather than a nation, it is a nation in the making. The effect of the régime is to impose a common pattern of life and a common culture on all the peoples from the Baltic to the Pacific. This culture pattern is not of purely Russian origin—it is a new mechanized and rationalized model which can be adopted by the former subject peoples of the Russian Empire without creating that feeling of racial inferiority which was inseparable from the process of Russification under the old régime.

Russians and Ukrainians, Tartars, Buriats, Georgians and Bashkirs all share on more or less equal terms in the new Soviet culture. And thus it prepares the way for the fusion of all these peoples in a new supernational unity.

Nevertheless this unity is not a cosmopolitan one: it is not the world civilization of the workers which was the original Communist ideal. It is a definite Eurasian unit which fuses together the two worlds of the Northern forest and the Eastern steppes, of Muscovy and Tartary, in a new technocratic society, ruled by new men for new ends. The fusion is still incomplete, but the last ten years seem to mark a decisive step in its development. There has been a deliberate attempt to create a Soviet patriotism and to restore the national traditions of culture in so far as these were not identified with the old ruling classes. At the same time there has been an attempt to recognize, at least in principle, the place of the peasants and the intelligentsia in the new society and to improve the lot of the peasantry, which had suffered so grievously during the period of collectivization. In these respects the Constitution of 1936 marked a turning point, not because it established democratic liberties in the Western sense, as Soviet sympathisers imagined, but, as Stalin himself explained in his report to the Soviet Congress, because of the obliteration of the social conflicts and contradictions that had marked the period of revolution. It was an official declaration of peace between the classes of the new society. Yet at the very moment when the new Constitution seemed to promise a new prospect of social peace, Russia was entering a new period of terrorism and repression, more severe than anything known in the past. From the end of 1934 there begins the series of wholesale purges which entirely changed the character of the Communist Party. The old Party leaders, like Bukharin, Radek and Zinoviev, were destroyed almost to a man, and after them in quick succession went the Communist exiles from Western Europe, the leaders of the constituent republics and the heads of the army and the G.P.U. No one was too influential or too unimportant to escape, and the fact that the vast majority of the accused admitted their guilt and accepted their condemnation with abject submissiveness gave a sinister impression of the irresistible power of the new autocracy.

The usual defence that has been offered for this new terror is that it was necessitated by external dangers and that it exterminated all the elements which might have been used as a Fifth Column by the enemies of the Communist régime. It is certainly true that the great purges were not unconnected with the rise of Nazi Germany and the growing threat to world peace both in the East and the West. But the reaction to Nazism and Fascism was not entirely negative. There was also an element of imitation which assimilated Communism to National Socialism, and transformed the Comintern into an instrument of Russian foreign policy.

This tendency became manifest in the face of Europe when in 1939 Stalin and Hitler made their momentous pact for the partition of Poland and the re-absorption of the Baltic States by the Russian Empire. At a single stroke the U.S.S.R. recovered the dominant position in Eastern Europe which the Tsarist Empire had occupied, and the territorial losses of the revolutionary period were almost completely restored. This diplomatic revolution, in spite of the laborious attempts of Communist propaganda to justify it, was in glaring contradiction to the accepted Communist policy of the previous period, and its substitution of the brutal realism of power politics for the political ideology of the "Common Front" against Fascism inevitably alienated the sympathies of the social idealists in Western Europe and America who had hitherto looked on the U.S.S.R. as the defender of democratic ideals against Hitler and Mussolini. Yet it did not save Russia from war and invasion, nor did it prevent the formation of a real common front between the U.S.S.R. and the Western powers, without which Stalin's power could hardly have survived.

The Allied victory brought Russia a greater increase of power and territory than any state has ever acquired. It led to the military occupation of the whole of Eastern and Central Europe as far west as Saxony and Eastern Austria, and to the creation of satellite Russian-dominated states in Poland, Czechoslovakia, Hungary, Rumania, Bulgaria and Albania. At the same time it strengthened Russian influence in Western Europe through the local Communist parties, which had won new influence and prestige through their share in the Resistance Movement against Germany.

Thus it seemed as though Russia was in a position to abandon its attitude of withdrawal and isolation, to turn its face once more to the West and to co-operate with America and Western Europe in the creation of a new international order. But this was not to be. No sooner had the war ended than the alliance with the Western powers began to break down. In spite of the enormous prestige and considerable popularity that the U.S.S.R enjoyed in the West during the later years of the war, it has steadily moved away from the West towards isolation, non-co-operation and open hostility, and this has inevitably led to a sharp anti-Russian and anti-Communist reaction in the West, above all in the U.S.A.

Moreover, great as the Western expansion of Russian power has been, it has been surpassed by the expansion of Russian influence in Asia. Even within the European zone of Soviet influence, Russia has already come up against the stubborn resistance of European nationalism at three key points—in Finland, in Yugoslavia and in Greece. But in Asia the victory of Communism in China is more far-reaching in its effects than even the conquest of Germany, and offers unlimited possibilities of further expansion in Indo-China, in Malaya, in Persia and perhaps in India. Consequently, Russia is tending at present to become the leader of the peoples of Asia and Africa in a crusade against Western imperialism, and the stronger this tendency becomes, the wider becomes the gulf between Russia and the West, and the more the Asiatic elements in Russian society and thought will be strengthened. Already Russia has ceased to be a European national state with an Asiatic empire, as she was in the nineteenth century, and has become a Eurasiatic world power which occupies the same strategic position—and very similar geographical limits—as the Mongol world empire of the thirteenth century.

But this vast expansion of power has brought Russia face to face with new problems and difficulties unlike anything she has known in the past. Hitherto the advance of Soviet power has been the work of a centralized dictatorship which has planned and organized everything from the centre and has permitted no differences of opinion and no independent centres of political action. None of the constituent states of the Soviet Union was in any way comparable to the R.S.F.S.R. which was the representative of the Great Russian people and of the Russian national tradition, and the same disproportion of size and strength characterizes the new satellite states that have been created in Eastern Europe. But with the victory of Communism in China, the U.S.S.R. is faced with the problem of an independent Communist state which far exceeds Soviet Russia herself in the number of its population and the strength and antiquity of its cultural tradition. Is China to become a centralized totalitarian state under its own independent dictatorship? Or is it to remain dependent on the Soviet system and on the dictatorship of the Kremlin as a new satellite state?

Neither of these solutions seems possible without imposing an enormous strain on the existing mechanism of the Soviet state and the Communist Party.

Moreover, is the Communist ideology strong enough to create a lasting social unity between peoples of such diverse character and culture and tradition as the Slavs of Eastern Europe, the Turks of Central Asia and the Chinese and the other peoples of the Far East? No doubt it does provide a bond between the revolutionary elements in different societies and cultures, but the situation is very different when Communism has attained power and when it is necessary to maintain unity not between irresponsible revolutionary groups but between governments and nations. Hitherto, and especially during the war years, the problem was solved by a growing emphasis on national patriotism and the historic Russian tradition, but this policy is obviously inapplicable to the new world situation in which Russia has become the champion of oriental nationalism and is being brought into ever closer association with the greatest of the Asiatic cultures. We have seen how for a thousand years Russia has oscillated between East and West, and to-day with the industrialization of Central Asia and the alliance with Communist China the orientalist tendency has become stronger than ever before. But even in its present state of weakness and disintegration European culture has not entirely lost its old power of attraction. The extension of Soviet power into the heart of Central Europe makes the separation of Russia from the West less complete than it was between the wars since, at least in Berlin and Vienna, the two worlds meet almost on equal terms.

CHAPTER VII

Asia and Europe

THERE has always been a tendency to regard Europe and Asia as the opposite poles of human civilization. It is an ancient tradition which goes back as far as the origins of European historiography, for Herodotus begins his story of the wars between the Persians and the Greeks with an excursion into the mythological origins of the feud. "For my part," he concludes, "I cannot conceive why these names, and especially women's names [Europe, Asia and Libya] should ever have been given to a tract which is in reality one, nor why the Nile and the Phasis [or according to others the Don and the Straits of Azov] should have been fixed on for the boundary lines. Nor can I even say who gave the three tracts their names or whence they took their titles." But in spite of his scepticism he does not question the reality of their historic opposition which gives his work its unity. The fact is that the territorial divisions of Europe and Asia have never entirely corresponded with their ideal forms or archetypes, and yet the latter have preserved their character and their influence through the ages, and even to-day, though their geographical meaning has entirely changed, Europe and Asia still seem to represent the same contrasting principles as they did in the time of Herodotus.

It was probably in the eighteenth and nineteenth centuries that this contrast was most sharply defined and most widely recognized. The following passage from a Victorian writer,

William Bodham Donne, may be taken as a typical expression of the traditional view at the moment when the supremacy and self-confidence of European civilization were still unchallenged.

"Europe is not the cradle of civilization—that had attained at least a high formed maturity on the banks of the Tigris, the Euphrates and the Nile ages before Agamemnon ruled at Mycenae or Theseus drew the demi of Attica within the precincts of a common wall. Neither to Europe do we owe the fontal precepts of religion and ethics, nor the germs of the arts which civilize life. In every one of these elements of social progression Asia and Egypt took the lead. But although neither the original parent nor the earliest nurse of civilization, Europe has been for nearly three thousand years that portion of the world which most actively, assiduously and successfully cherished, advanced and perfected these rudiments of moral, intellectual and political cultivation. Of civil freedom it was the birthplace; neither of the older continents, however mature may have been its peculiar civilization, has ever possessed, without the aid of European contact and example, a community of free men, who distinguished the obedience that is due to law from the subservience which is paid to a master. And possessing civil freedom, at least among its nobler and governing races, Europe has carried to a higher stage of development every lesson and every art which it derived from other regions, and elevated the type and standard of humanity itself. Asia and Africa have generally receded from and, in the majority of their races, lost sight of entirely, the paths and the conditions of progressive civilization. In these regions, man is a weed. He is ruled in masses; he thinks in masses. His institutions, histories and modes of faith are unchanged through almost immemorial tracts of time. . . ."[1]

To-day the situation has been entirely altered by the rise of oriental nationalism and the revolutionary changes in Asiatic civilization which have taken place within the life-time of the present generation, as well as by the develop-ment of the economic and political power of the New World. And when to these factors are added the successive blows which the World Wars have inflicted on European power and prestige, it may well seem as though Europe was likely to lose not only her old position of world hegemony but even her autonomy, and was destined to be re-absorbed by the teeming millions of the oriental world.

Nevertheless, in spite of these revolutionary changes, the traditional contrast between European and Asiatic civiliza-tion still subsists. Asia is still the domain of vast, anonymous, mass civilizations, while Europe still preserves a higher level of political self-consciousness and a stronger sense of per-sonality and of the rights and values that depend on person-ality than anywhere else in the world, even than America, which has during the last hundred years moved so rapidly in the direction of a new type of mass civilization. But the modern contrast between Europe and Asia can no longer be expressed in the Victorian or Hellenic terms of progress and stagnation or civilization and barbarism. The same terms are used in both continents—civilization and progress, demo-cracy and nationality, liberty and humanity—but the terms have a different content. Take the case of nationality, which at first sight seems a relatively objective concept. The idea of nationality plays a no less important part in modern

[1] Smith's *Dictionary of Greek and Roman Geography,* s.v. "Europa," 1854. It is interesting to see how in the heyday of nineteenth-century Romanticism the ideas and the style of the eighteenth century still survive.

Asia than in Europe, but it means something entirely different. The nations of Europe are relatively small social units co-existing in a common cultural tradition. The nationalities of Asia are vast cultural unities which correspond to Europe itself rather than to the nations of Europe. The intimate relation between state, nation and language which has determined the whole idea of nationality in Europe and which still subsists to-day has never been characteristic of Asia.

In India, for example, we find peoples with their own history and languages and literatures, some of great antiquity, like the Tamils and Kanarese in the south, and yet they are not reckoned as nations, but merely as provinces or sectors of the Indian people. And the fact that the Asiatic nations are civilizations or cultural autarchies has its corollary in the fact that Asia itself has no cultural unity. There is a European culture even though this has never entirely corresponded with the European continent, but there is no Asiatic culture. From time immemorial Asia has been divided into a number of civilizations which are as distinct from one another as they are from Europe, which in the past have been almost closed worlds to one another, and possess independent traditions of culture reaching back behind the dawn of history and before the birth of Europe. In so far as Asia has a common life or a common consciousness, it has received it during the last hundred years from Europe, either by the communication of modern ideas or by reaction against European imperialism. It is true that there are intermediate zones of mixed culture between the great civilizations of Asia, such as Indo-China and East Turkestan and the East Indies, but this is the inevitable result of the tendency of a culture to influence the regions with which it is in contact—a tendency which is seen in the prehistoric cultures of Egypt and Mesopotamia no less than in the civilizations of the modern world.

From the standpoint of the history of culture, it would be better if we could speak of the Asias rather than Asia. In the first place there is the Far East, which had its centre of origin in the valley of the Yellow River and which has spread eastward to Korea and Japan and southward to Southern China and Indo-China. Secondly there is India, with its centre in the valleys of the Indus and the Ganges, which has spread southward to Ceylon and south-east to Cambodia and Java. Thirdly there is South-Western Asia, which has united a number of ancient traditions of culture into the religious and cultural unity of Islam and which has expanded in all directions—westward and southward into Africa, northward to the Black Sea and the Volga, and east-ward into India and Malaya. Finally there is Northern Asia, into which Russia has expanded as though it were an his-torical vacuum but which in the Middle Ages was the domain of the Mongol world power, the last and greatest of a long succession of nomad empires which had ebbed and flowed through the northern steppes for centuries, leaving their debris like stranded ships, not only in Central Asia, but in Eastern and South-Eastern Europe as far west as Hungary.

Of these four areas, three still possess their own tradi-tions of religion and philosophy. Each has its own sacred language, its own classical literature and its own tradition of law. They are essentially the civilizations of Confu-cianism, Hinduism and Islam. Their education and thought have been formed and nourished effectively by the Chinese classics, the Vedanta and the Koran, and their behaviour has been conditioned in a hundred ways by the rites and customs and ceremonial forms which equally form part of these socio-religious traditions. In short, the great Asiatic civilizations are *ways of life* in a much more definite and conscious sense than that of any national Western culture. The whole civilization is penetrated from top to bottom by the same system of ideas, so that a man can give theological or metaphysical reasons for the way in which he cooks his dinner or washes his face, as well as for the forms in which he prays and the principles by which he guides his conduct.

Of course this only applies to the past, for at the present time all the oriental cultures are being subjected to a process of revolutionary change which is sweeping away the old landmarks, criticizing the old standards and often destroying the old creeds and dogmas. In the last thirty years the progress of Western civilization in Asia has been more rapid than ever before. The influence of the machine—the motor, the aeroplane, the Bren gun, the cinema and the radio—and of mechanized industry have had a far more powerful and direct effect on the mind of the masses than all the efforts of Western administrators and missionaries for the last two hundred years. And the fact that the control of these new forces has passed from European imperialism to oriental nationalism increases their power, since they now act from within oriental society and find their chief support among the leaders of the nationalist reaction. Thus the modern nationalist movements in Asia contain a principle of internal conflict which is due to the historical circumstances under which they arose. They are at once the result of the influence of European ideas and of a reaction against the political hegemony of Europe. They have arisen and flourished among the intelligentsia which has been educated in Europe or under European influences and has revolted against its cultural tradition in the spirit of nineteenth-century liberalism or twentieth-century socialism. But it is impossible to abolish in a generation forms of thought and habits of conduct which have reigned unchallenged for thousands of years. They still form the judgment and the taste and the imagination of the whole people, even though the more superficial organs of public opinion like the press and the political parties seem completely indoctrinated with alien ideas. Thus there are two alternatives open to Asiatic nationalism. It may follow the same path as that of the West and create a mechanized secular culture which will be able to meet that of the West as an equal in the same field. Or it may, like Gandhi, return to its cultural tradition and reassert the ultimate archetypal forms of his own civilization against Western ideas and techniques as well as against the more obvious forms of Western imperialism. But if this path is chosen, the process of cosmopolitanism which marked the period of European predominance will be discarded and the old traditions of the autonomous and autochthonous Asiatic cultures will return in a new form.

In either case the fact that these cultures are regarded—at least in the case of India and China—as nationalities or national states is bound to have revolutionary effects on world politics and on the character of international society. The society of nations is a European idea which was developed within the narrow limits of Western Christendom, long before the days of railways and steamships and aeroplanes and wireless telegraphy. The great powers were states with a population of ten to twenty million inhabitants, and little states like Holland and Denmark were strong enough to play an independent part in international affairs. And even to-day the pattern of international relations has not been altered in theory, although the advent of the new massive world powers like the United States and Soviet Russia has profoundly altered the actual distribution of power. But if the weight of the immense mass civilizations of Asia, with their populations of four hundred millions apiece, is thrown into the scales, the balance will be completely altered. There is no common standard by which we can measure states of one and a half to three and a half millions like New Zealand and Norway and Denmark and states of three hundred and fifty to four hundred and fifty millions like India and China. If we measure them by the juridical standard of the equality of sovereign states, we do an injustice to the oriental civilizations which are so much more than states; while if we adopt the quantitative standard of size and population, we shall do an equal injustice to the small European nations which have achieved such a high standard of political liberty and social welfare by their own unaided powers. Judged as mass powers they are pigmies by the side of giants, judged as political societies they are men by the side of children. The greatness of the oriental nationalities does not rest on their political achievements, but on the riches of their cultural heritage and on their inexhaustible resources of manpower.

Up to the present, however, these resources have not been developed, even to the extent that those of the most backward Western countries have been. Southern and Eastern Asia are the most poverty-stricken regions of the globe. Human life is cheap; man is often a beast of burden, and the masses live so near the starvation line that a bad season or a sudden inundation will destroy more human beings than a major European war. It is obvious that under such conditions the political institutions and the social ideals that were created by the privileged classes of privileged communities are inapplicable. In other words democracy, equality and the rights of man have a very different meaning in the East and the West, and the fact that the politically active classes of the East have been to school with the West and have borrowed Western political ideologies and social ideals without essential modifications only increases the difficulty. A similar problem arose in the nineteenth century when the ideology of revolutionary liberalism was imported ready-made into Spanish America by a Creole minority which had little in common with the uneducated masses of the population. But the problems of Latin America were on a much smaller scale, owing to the centrifugal character of Spanish republicanism, whereas in Asia nationalism, both Indian and Chinese, has a strong tendency towards unity though it is not always powerful enough to withstand the disruptive influence of communal rivalry and provincial separation. The organization of a modern national state with a population of four hundred millions is a colossal task even under the most favourable conditions. It involves an immense concentration of power, and there is a danger that when such a concentration has been achieved, it will be directed not so much towards the solution of internal social problems as towards external aggression and conquest. We have seen a notable example of this tendency in the case of modern Japan, which was the first Asiatic state to adopt modern nationalist ideals. And if the greater civilizations of China and India were to follow the same path—as China gives strong hints that she means to do—it would be a disaster for the cause of international peace and the future of humanity.

The obvious rational solution of the problem is to be found in a new system of co-operation between East and West in which Europe and America provide the economic assistance and the scientific and technological guidance which are necessary in order to develop the resources and raise the standard of life in Asia without interfering with the political or cultural independence of the Eastern peoples.

But there is an element of fanaticism and xenophobia in oriental nationalism which is apt to resent any suggestion of Western control and to look with suspicion on the West even when it is bringing gifts. This xenophobia is rooted in the deep subsoil of ancient cultural traditions. It is a protest against a threat to the oriental way of life and its religious background which is often strongest amongst those who are least conscious of it and which can only be overcome when the representatives of the highest culture in East and West meet face to face.[1] Unfortunately the co-operation between East and West which is so essential for the solution of economic problems in Asia does not take place on this cultural level. The technological self-assertion of the Western expert meets the political self-assertion of oriental nationalism without finding any medium for cultural and spiritual understanding. And it is this situation which is most favourable to the spread of Communism, since the decision to eliminate the old cultural and religious traditions alike in the East and the West makes it possible for the oriental nationalist to meet the Western technologist on the basis of a common materialism.

But though both parties may feel that they are victorious, their victory has been won not over one another but over their own spiritual traditions and their own cultural roots. In this respect there is little to distinguish the new ideology from the Western Liberal ideal of the unification of the world by free trade and the progress of science and industry. It is in fact a proletarian version of the same gospel of material progress, which arose in Europe in the eighteenth century. This ideology may provide a temporary bond between certain active political elements in the East and the West, but it does not touch the deeper spiritual issues between their cultures and consequently it does not provide a basis for the construction of a true world culture.

[1] Cf. the striking account of the meeting of East and West on the level of the higher culture in nineteenth-century Bengal, given by Mr. N. Chaudahuri in his *Autobiography of an Unknown Indian* (Macmillan, 1951).

CHAPTER VIII

Europe Overseas: Colonization and Empire

THE change in the world position of Europe which has taken place during the last fifty years has inevitably caused a strong reaction against the spirit of nineteenth-century imperialism. The idea of empire has become identified with the oppression of subject peoples, the "White Man's Burden" has become a joke, and the whole colonial development is regarded as a form of economic exploitation. Yet the imperialist phase of Western culture is not confined to the second half of the nineteenth century. It was the culmination of a much wider movement which goes back to the close of the Middle Ages and which has been one of the main forces in the formation of the modern world. However great may be our moral disapproval of *Homo Europaeus* in his relations with weaker and more primitive peoples, we cannot ignore his positive achievements, for they have changed the face of the earth and created a new world, or even a number of new worlds. Moreover, this question has a peculiar importance for the English-speaking peoples, in the Old and the New Worlds. For the United States, which have always been foremost in the denunciation of imperialism and colonialism, are themselves the greatest product of these movements; while Great Britain has been in the past the greatest of all the colonial powers and still owes her international importance to her imperial position.

But leaving aside these considerations, it is impossible to understand the nature of the modern world apart from the

Western movement of colonial expansion which has transformed the closed Mediterranean continental world of ancient and mediaeval culture into an oceanic civilization which has unified the world. Whatever may be our moral judgment on Imperialism, we must accept it, like War or the State, as one of the constituent elements that have made the modern world. Moreover, even when we consider it from a strictly moral point of view, we must recognize its mixed character. Like civilization itself, it has been inspired by ideal as well as material motives and has had a missionary as well as an acquisitive character. It has brought out both the best and the worst elements in Western culture.

This two-fold character goes back to the very origins of the movement in the later mediaeval period. For the great discoveries which were the starting-point of the European expansion were themselves inspired by a double motive. They were an attempt to free European commerce from the stranglehold imposed by the Turkish conquest of the Levant and they were an extension and continuation of the crusading movement which played such a great part in the history of mediaeval Christendom. This second motive is especially clear in the work of Prince Henry of Portugal, who was the great precursor of the Age of Discovery. In view of the repeated failures of the crusading movement, and especially of the latest crusading efforts of Portugal in Morocco, Prince Henry conceived the idea of turning the flank of Islam by the exploration of West Africa and the establishment of a new Christian dominion in Guinea. The indomitable persistence with which he pursued this limited aim launched Portugal on the path of discovery which led ultimately to the circumnavigation of the Cape of Good Hope in 1486 and to the opening of the route to India and the Far East in 1492. The same motives led Ferdinand and Isabella to finance the voyage of Columbus in 1492, and it is no accident that the discovery of America was the immediate sequel to the capture of Granada, which ended the long history of the Spanish Reconquest. Yet from the beginning the economic motive played a great part in the movement. Henry the Navigator himself encouraged the African slave-trade, and the famous letter of Toscanelli to Canon Fernan Martins of Lisbon, which is said to have given Columbus the idea of his Western route, is not inspired by any crusading idealism but with the concrete problem of finding "a shorter way to the place of spices".

Thus the discovery of the New World and the opening of the new route to India were at once the result of the old mediaeval crusading ideal and of a very modern interest in cheaper grocery, and this combination of incongruous motives characterizes the whole history of the European colonial development. The conquest of America was the work of predatory adventurers and devoted missionaries, partially controlled by a remote government, which was itself divided and frustrated by the conflict between its sense of Christian responsibility and its lust for power and wealth. On the whole it was the higher motive which determined the broad lines of imperial policy, and the New Laws for the Indies, which express the principles and aims of the Spanish Empire, show a remarkably high sense of responsibility for the welfare of the native population and a far-reaching concern for the creation of a Christian society and culture in the New World.

Nevertheless there was a tremendous gulf between the high principles and ideals of the government at Madrid and Seville and the interests and behaviour of the men on the spot, and in order to control the latter the government established an elaborate machinery of centralized control which was both costly and cumbrous. The resultant conflict between the Spanish-born lawyers and ecclesiastics who represented the government and the colonial population which had to do the actual work of conquest and settlement remained a great weakness of Spanish imperialism and the ultimate cause of its downfall. Moreover, the high ideals of the Spanish government did not prevent it from claiming the lion's share in the profits of colonial enterprise. The treasures of the Indies, especially after the opening of the great silver mines at Potosi in 1545, were the mainstay of Spanish finances, and they were used not for the development of the colonial empire, but to provide the sinews of war at home. Thus the American empire remained perennially starved of men and money and was never able to develop the trade and industry that its natural resources demanded.

The Portuguese Empire suffered from similar defects. Its original creation was an even more remarkable achievement than the Spanish conquest of America, since Vasco da Gama and Albuquerque had to overcome the resistance of highly civilized peoples who were in many respects more advanced than the Europeans themselves. The successful conquest of the historic trade centres of the East, of Goa and Malacca and Hormuz, with minute fleets operating thousands of miles from their base, was a miracle of heroism and strategy. It was inspired by the same crusading ideal as that of Henry the Navigator, since it was an extension of his project for turning the flanks of Islam and creating a new Christian empire in the East. But the gap between principles and practice was even wider than that of the Spanish Empire, since it was harder for Lisbon to establish effective control over its immense chain of possessions which reached from West Africa and Brazil to India and the Moluccas. These ideals were never entirely forgotten. Indeed it was the Portuguese Empire which was the pioneer of Christianity in Eastern Asia and opened the way for men like St. Francis Xavier and St. John Britto, who were among the greatest missionaries of any age. Yet their failure was equally apparent, and it was St. Francis Xavier himself who passed judgment on them when he wrote to King John III: "Experience has taught me that Your Highness has no power in India for the spread of the faith of Christ, but only to carry off and enjoy all the temporal riches of the country.... Because I know what goes on here, I have no hope that commands or rescripts sent in favour of Christianity will be fulfilled in India; and therefore I am almost fleeing to Japan not to waste any more time."[1]

But whatever the intentions of the government, the forces at its disposal were far too weak for this immense task, and the effort to sustain the burden of empire exhausted both the physical and moral resources of the nation.

Thus, after the union of Portugal with Spain in 1580, there was a rapid decline of Portuguese power, which ultimately lost its control of the seas and of the oriental trade routes to the Dutch.

The Dutch colonial empire differed from that of its predecessors by its purely commercial character. The United Provinces were the first bourgeois state of modern Europe. They were concerned not with the old ideas of a crusade against the infidel or with the conversion of the heathen but with practical problems of trade and dividends. It was not even a question of trade following the flag, for the flag was simply the ensign of the great trading companies: the East India Company, the West India Company and the rest. But this very limitation of aims made for efficiency and the adaptation of means to ends. The recklessness with which crusaders and conquistadors had squandered blood and treasure was replaced by the merchants' careful calculation of profit and loss. It is true that the Dutch East

[1] *Monumenta Xaveriana I,* 507–12.

India Company was no less ruthless in its exploitation of the native population than its Spanish and Portuguese predecessors, but it never conquered for the sake of empire. It did not lose a man or a ship unless there was a reasonable chance of a clear profit to the stockholders.

The result was that the Dutch became for a time the masters of the seas and the pioneers of world trade and finance. Throughout Europe the mercantile system took the place of the crusading ideal as the primary motive of colonial expansion. Since national power depended on national wealth and national wealth depended on trade, it was the duty of a statesman to see that his state acquired the largest possible share in the total volume of world trade. Colonies, plantations and factories[1] were as much a part of the apparatus of national power as armies and fortresses, and it was as important for the statesman to watch over them and develop them as it was for a householder to cultivate his estate and to attend to his business. Consequently the statesmen and political economists of that age had as strong a sense of the primacy of the economic motive and the necessity of a competitive struggle for international markets between states as the capitalists and economists of the following age had for the process of competition and the dominance of the profit motive among individuals. In both cases moral and religious considerations tended to be ignored or set aside in favour of a purely rational criterion of economic gain and loss.

The spirit of the mercantile system was most completely represented by Holland, where the merchants and the capitalists were the rulers of the state and where the whole social organism was dominated by the economic motive. But the other colonial powers, especially France and England, accepted the same principles and applied them

[1] i.e. trading establishments in foreign territory under the control of a "factor".

in a more systematic form and on an even larger scale, as we see above all in the work of Colbert which was the most ambitious scheme of empire-building on mercantile principles ever conceived by a single mind. His plans were, however, frustrated by the fact that he served a king and a state dominated by military and religious rather than economic motives. The interests of the French colonial empire were always subordinated to those of European power politics, a process which reached its logical conclusion when Napoleon sold Louisiana to the United States for fifteen million dollars.

Thus it was Britain and not France which gained the most benefit from the Dutch example and became the heir of the Dutch commercial empire. But the British Empire differed from its rivals by its diversity and by the slow and tentative character of its growth. The great instrument of its development was the chartered joint-stock company, which goes back to the creation of the Russia Company in 1555 and had its origins in the tradition of the later mediaeval trading companies, such as the Merchant Adventurers. But the great English innovation was the use of the chartered company for purposes of colonization and settlement as well as trade, and from the foundation of Virginia in 1606 and of the Massachusetts Bay Company in 1629 the colonies of settlement played as great a part in the development of the Empire as the purely trading companies like the East India Company, which was founded in 1600, two years before that of its great Dutch rival. The colonies of settlement naturally had more in common with the Spanish type of colonial development than with the Dutch, and as with the former, religious motives played an important part in their history. It is true that the missionary activities of the English colonists were weak and unsuccessful; but as a motive for colonization among the settlers themselves, religion played a larger part than in any of the European colonial movements.[1] Above all in New England, but also in Maryland and Pennsylvania and to a certain extent in Georgia in the eighteenth century, the English colonies became a refuge for religious minorities in search of religious freedom, and though the proportion of these ideological emigrants to the total population was not large, they had a very important influence on the character of colonial society.

Nevertheless the colonies in the temperate zone, which were most suited to European colonization, were not the most important from the point of view of imperial policy. Mercantilist theory was not favourable to overseas settlement for its own sake. Its whole emphasis was on trade which, as Defoe wrote, "is the wealth of the World" and whose "fruitful progeny were manufacture and navigation." Colonies existed only to increase the wealth of the nation by increasing its trade, and any form of competition between the colony and the mother country must be discouraged by the laws of trade and navigation. Consequently mercantilism favoured the establishment of tropical colonies, whose products did not compete with those of the mother country, or trading establishments like that of the East India Company, which directly increased England's share in world trade. Thus the Empire was conceived as a vast trading concern which would absorb the greatest possible amount of the world's wealth and afford employment to the largest possible number of British ships and men. But since these ideas were also shared by the other colonial powers, especially Holland and France, they led to an intensive process of commercial competition and to a bitter struggle for

[1] This religious influence also existed in the French colonial empire, above all in the foundation of Montreal, which is one of the most remarkable examples of religious idealism in colonial history. Moreover, Canada was also the scene of the most heroic missionary activity. But historical circumstances limited the success of both these movements.

colonial and sea power which characterized the second half of the seventeenth and the whole of the eighteenth century. At the same time it led to the great commercial "interests" like those of the West Indian sugar plantations, the West African slave-trade and the East India Company, which exerted a great but unwholesome influence on English politics.

It was during this century and a half that Western imperialism acquired the evil reputation which it has never entirely succeeded in living down, and which has tainted the expansion of Western culture with a spirit of exploitation and acquisitiveness. As Sir Charles Lucas wrote: "What killed the old Empire was dominance of trade in its most vicious, insolent and godless guise, exulting in the appalling wickedness of the slave traffic, instilling poison into the heart of the Empire, from the West through the West India interest, from the East through the nabobs. . . . In the course of the friction and strife that tore the Empire asunder, on one point and another there were many and strong points to be made for Great Britain; but at the back of it all was the fundamental mischief that the outlook of the Empire had been distorted by trade; that trade carried to hideous lengths had caused the English genius for making new homes and carrying liberties across the seas to be held suspect, and had deadened the call of religion."[1]

Yet already in the eighteenth century we see the beginnings, and more than the beginnings, of a moral reaction.

The victory of Great Britain over her rivals in the colonial conflict which was achieved at the end of the Seven Years War (1756–63) did not mean the victory of the mercantilist ideals. On the contrary, it was followed by a series of changes which transformed the character of the Empire and

[1] Sir Charles Lucas, K.C.B., K.C.M.G., *Religion, Colonization and Trade: The Driving Forces of the Old Empire*, pp. 74–5 (1930).

the ideological basis of colonial policy. On the one hand, the conquest of Canada freed the English colonies in North America from their dependence on the military support of the mother country and accentuated the divergence between their economic interests and British commercial policy, so that they had both the motive and the power to assert their independence. On the other hand, the victory over the French in India forced Great Britain to abandon the limited commercial aims of the old East India Company and to accept an increasing measure of responsibility for the government of vast oriental territories and populations. At the same time, the economic principles on which the old colonial system rested were discarded by the Physiocrats in France and by Adam Smith and his followers in Great Britain, and their place was taken by the new philosophy of economic liberalism which taught that the wealth of nations was to be found in free trade, freedom of individual enterprise and competition and the abolition of the old restrictive laws of trade and navigation. This movement of economic liberalism was accompanied by, and to some extent related to, the general movement of humanitarian reform which caused a strong reaction against the moral abuses of the old system, above all against the slave-trade and the oppression of subject peoples. On the Continent this reaction expressed itself in works like the Abbé Raynal's *History of the Indies*,[1] which achieved immense popularity, and finally in the liberal idealism of the revolutionary period. In England, on the other hand, it became associated with the religious revival

---

[1] *Histoire philosophique et politique des établissements et des commerce des Européens dans les deux Indes.* Amsterdam, 1770, 4 vols. English trans. 1776. This was a co-operative work which owed a great deal to the collaboration of Diderot and d'Holbach. In spite of the efforts of the censorship to suppress it, it spread all over Europe in numerous editions and translations and was one of the most successful of all the works of Encyclopaedist propaganda. The author used part of his profits to found prizes for a discussion on whether the discovery of America had been a misfortune for Europe!

of the later eighteenth century and bore fruit in popular movements for practical humanitarian reform of which the great crusade against slavery and the slave-trade is the most famous. Even more important, though more gradual in its effects, was the rise of the Protestant missions, which were destined to have as great an influence on the British Empire in the nineteenth century as the Catholic missions had on the Spanish and Portuguese empires in the sixteenth.

The ultimate effect of these changes was to transform the character of the Empire and the spirit of its policy. On the one hand, men lost faith in the economic doctrines of mercantilism on which the old Empire had been based; while on the other, they acquired new religious and humanitarian ideals and a sense of world mission which appealed especially to the new middle classes that were taking an increasingly important place in English social and intellectual life.

But these changes were slow to take effect. The immediate cause of the transformation of the Empire was the tremendous ordeal of the wars of the American and French Revolutions, which lasted with intermissions for nearly fifty years. Throughout this period the dominant issue was not commercial interests but military and naval power. Canada became the refuge of the displaced persons from the United States—The United Empire Loyalists; New South Wales was founded as a convict settlement, and Wellesley created a new Empire in India. At the same time, the old colonial empires collapsed. The Dutch East India Company came to an end, the French colonial empire was liquidated, while the Spanish Empire, the first, greatest and most ancient of them all, was on its death-bed.

Thus everything favoured the extension of British colonial power, and it was in fact during this period that the old colonial system was transformed into a world Empire, based

on the control of the seas and reaching from Africa to
Malaya and from Newfoundland to New South Wales. But
in this new Empire the colonies of settlement with their self-
governing institutions played little or no part. Neither the
humanitarian reformers nor the soldiers were sympathetic
to the colonists. In this respect Wellington, who himself
played so large a part in the building and government of the
new Empire, is typical. In spite of his intense loyalty to the
imperial tradition, he had little sympathy for the British
colonist and was always firmly opposed to allowing any
settlement of Europeans among the native population. As
he once wrote to Charles Wynne, "You are not aware here
[in England] of the infirmity of the European (particularly
British) character and of its consequences in all relations of
life. Rely upon it that with all our civilization and advantages we are the nation in Europe the least disciplined and
the least to be trusted in a situation in which we are not
controlled by the strong arm of authority and law."[1]

During the half-century between the loss of the American
colonies and the Reform Bill (1782–1832), this ideal of "the
strong arm of authority and law" was the dominant spirit
in the organization of the Empire. It was a naval and
military Empire, governed by soldiers like Carleton and
Prevost in Canada, Cornwallis and Hastings in India,
D'Urban and Sir Harry Smith in South Africa, Maitland—
"King Tom"—in Ceylon and the Mediterranean, and Mac-
quarie, Gipps and Arthur in Australia. This predominance
of military considerations is shown by the fact that the
colonial department throughout this period and down to
1854 was attached to the War Office.

Nevertheless this did not prevent the new humanitarian
and religious movements from exerting an influence on

---

[1] Letter to the Hon. C. Wynne, Nov. 11, 1826. *Despatches,* 3rd series,
Vol. III, p. 450.

colonial policy. Indeed there has never been a time when religious idealism played so important a part in the development of the Empire. This was due above all to the action of the able and devoted group of Evangelicals, known as the Clapham Sect, who were led by Wilberforce and Henry Thornton, and included such men as the elder James Stephen and the elder Charles Grant, Zachary Macaulay, John Shore and Edward Eliot. Although the primary concern of this group was the suppression of the slave-trade and the abolition of slavery itself, they had a far-reaching interest in everything that concerned the spread of Christianity and the protection of native peoples from European exploitation. All of them were men of affairs; most of them were Tory members of Parliament in close relation with the governments of Pitt and Liverpool, while some of them took a responsible part in the government of the Empire, like Charles Grant, who was Chairman of the East India Company, Sir John Shore, who was Governor-General of Bengal, and Zachary Macaulay, who was the founder and first governor of Sierra Leone, our first African colony. But perhaps their most important contribution to the Empire was made in the following generation through their sons, like the younger Charles Grant, Lord Glanely, who was colonial secretary from 1835 to 1839, and above all the younger James Stephen (1787–1859), who was for more than a generation the power behind the scenes at the Colonial Office and who did more than any other single individual to determine the character and organize the administration of the new Empire during the crucial period of its development.

James Stephen was a man of great integrity and high ideals with an enormous capacity for work, but he was no imperialist. He regarded the Empire as a burden which must be carried in the service of humanity and Christian civilization, rather than as an instrument for national expansion and power. Though he believed in the White Man's Burden, he did not believe in the white man as colonist and empire-builder, unless he was controlled by "the strong arm of authority and law".

But in these respects he did not go so far as the official leaders of the humanitarian movement like Sir T. F. Buxton and the missionaries like Dr. Philip, who had a considerable influence on government policy in the 'thirties. It was they who were responsible for the report of the Select Committee on the Treatment of Aborigines, in 1837, which is perhaps the strongest indictment of the evils of European colonization that has ever been published by a European government. It is also the most remarkable expression of the religious idealism which inspired the Clapham Sect and the Evangelical movement of humanitarian reform, since it bases its recommendations on strictly theological considerations. "The British Empire," it declares, "has been signally blessed by Providence, and her eminence, her strength, her wealth, her prosperity, her intellectual, her moral and her religious advantages, are so many reasons for peculiar obedience to the laws of Him who guides the destinies of nations. These were given for some higher purpose than commercial prosperity and military renown. . . . He who has made Great Britain what she is, will enquire of our hands how we have employed the influence He has lent to us in our dealings with the untutored and defenceless savage; whether it has been engaged in seizing their lands, warring upon their people, and transplanting unknown disease and deeper degradation through the remote regions of the earth; or whether we have as far as we have been able, informed their ignorance, and invited and afforded them the opportunity of becoming partakers of that civilization, that innocent commerce, that knowledge and that faith with which it has pleased a gracious Providence to bless our own country".[1]

The report was mainly concerned with conditions in South Africa, but also included New Zealand, Australia and the Pacific, and in every case it reached the conclusion that the cause of the natives was an imperial responsibility which could not safely be entrusted to the European colonist, and that so far as possible the land should be left to the natives and the natives to the missionaries, who were "to form schemes for advancing their social and political improvement".

The missionaries were not, however, in a position to discharge such a function effectively. All the British missionary societies were of recent origin[2] and their missionaries were for the most part men of humble origin and scanty education who were quite unfitted to grapple with the complex problems arising from the clash of cultures and the reactions of tribal societies to religious and economic change. It is true that some of them were men of outstanding character like William Carey (1761–1834), the Baptist village cobbler, who went to India in 1792 as the pioneer of British missionary enterprise, John Williams (1796–1839), the London mechanic, who achieved such a remarkable success in the Pacific, and Robert Moffat (1795–1883), who spent his life in the service of the Bechuana and the other native peoples of South Africa. But it is not surprising that their championship of the cause of the subject peoples, and still more the propaganda of their supporters in England as represented by Exeter Hall, should have aroused the bitter hostility of the other interested parties—the Boers in South Africa, the

---

[1] Bell and Morrell, *British Colonial Policy, 1830–60. Select Documents,* p. 546.
[2] The Baptist Missionary Society was founded in 1792, and the Scottish Missionary Society, the London Missionary Society and the Church Missionary Society all belong to the same decade.

settlers in New Zealand, the traders in West Africa and the Pacific and the planters in the West Indies.

It was in this situation, characterized by an authoritarian government, a humanitarian public opinion and a discontented colonial population, that a new movement of colonial reform arose, led by Charles Buller, Gilbert Wakefield and Sir W. Molesworth. It was equally hostile to the authoritarianism of the Colonial Office and to the humanitarianism of Exeter Hall and was inspired by the Elizabethan, or rather Jacobean, ideals of plantation by chartered companies and of the creation of a new Britain beyond the seas. Its importance is due not so much to Wakefield's plan of systematic colonization, which was only carried out successfully in the single case of the Canterbury Settlement in New Zealand, but rather to the revival of interest that it produced in the whole question of migration and overseas settlement and to its optimistic attitude to the Empire and to colonial expansion. The Colonial Reformers were not imperialists in the later nineteenth-century sense; they included Liberals like Molesworth and Grote, who regarded colonial self-government as the first step towards ultimate independence and who conceived the British expansion, not in the Roman imperial spirit, but after the Greek model, as a swarming off of free daughter communities which would reproduce the social structure of the parent society in a new environment. Nevertheless they were the creators of the *mystique* of nineteenth-century British imperialism, with its belief in the colonial genius of the Anglo-Saxon race and the limitless possibilities of world expansion.

There is indeed a much closer affinity between nineteenth-century imperialism and the liberal tradition in England than is usually recognized. Lord Durham, who was the patron of the Colonial Reformers and whose plan of constitutional development in Canada was the prelude

to the restoration of colonial self-government, was one of
the leading radicals of his time. And the men who carried
on the work of the Colonial Reformers in the following
generation, like Dilke and Seeley, who did so much to
popularize the idea of empire, were also Liberals. But
at the same time, the dominant current of Liberal opinion
remained indifferent to the colonial idea and regarded
the Empire as a burden.[1] The reaction against mercantilist
ideas reached its climax in the middle of the century,
with the repeal of the Corn Laws in 1846 and of the
Navigation Laws in 1849, and thenceforward for twenty
years English Liberalism was dominated by the ideal of
universal Free Trade and a free world market. Yet this
movement, in spite of its cosmopolitan ideology, was in
reality closely connected with the imperial development. The
new Empire which had been built up during the Napoleonic
wars, with its control of the seas and its network of strategic
bases, provided the political framework on which the commercial expansion of nineteenth-century England was based.
The extension of this system by the establishment of the
free port of Singapore in 1819, the annexation of Hong
Kong in 1842 and of Aden in 1837–39, secured the control
of the great trade route to Asia and the development of
British trade with China. British coal, British engineering
and British steamships were the common factors on which
the expansion of the British Empire and the development of
British world trade were based. To the average Englishman
the Empire meant the system of organized security under
which the investor, the trader, the planter, the prospector
and the missionary could be free to carry on their various
activities. And since this system was no longer based on
the principle of commercial monopoly, but on the extension

[1] As John Bright once declared, with reference to West Africa, "Fresh
acquisitions of territory add to the burdens of the people of Great Britain
and Ireland. We take the burden and we pay the charge."

of world trade, there was no necessary conflict between the economic idealism of Free Trade and the political realities of imperial control. The Victorians believed quite sincerely that the opening of the world to European trade was a moral duty as well as an economic advantage, as we see from the writings of the nineteenth-century missionaries like John Williams in the Pacific and David Livingstone in Africa. Livingstone above all was convinced that the only way to stop the slave-trade was by opening Africa to British trade as well as to Christian missions, and since both these forces required peace and security for their development, he was also a supporter and pioneer of imperial expansion. To men like Livingstone the expansion of the Empire meant the extension of Christendom, and they still believed that European culture with all its faults and injustices represented a higher form of human civilization on which all the hopes of the world for liberty and progress rested.[1]

In the second half of the nineteenth century the whole situation was altered by the extension to the colonial world of the national rivalries of continental Europe. The cosmopolitan idealism of the Free Traders had given place to the economic nationalism which found its first expression in Frederick List's *National System of Political Economy* (1884) and which was in effect a new version of the old mercantilist doctrines adapted to the needs of modern industrialism. It was this neo-mercantilism which led to the scramble for colonial territories as the sources of raw materials and which was responsible for some of the ugliest features of modern European imperialism. The British Empire was not primarily responsible for this development, which actually produced its worst fruits in the regions that did not fall to the share of any of the great powers, such as the no-man's-

[1] See his concluding remarks in *Journeys and Researches in South Africa*, Ch. XXXII (1857).

land of the Putumayo in South America, and above all the Congo Free State, which had been founded under the humanitarian auspices of an International Association for the Suppression of the Slave Trade! Nevertheless both the new imperialism and the new mercantilism inevitably produced a strong reaction on British imperial policy and were largely responsible for the change from the cautious paternalism of Sir James Stephen to the expansionist imperialism of Joseph Chamberlain.

Chamberlain, like Durham and the Colonial Reformers, was a radical by tradition and had a stronger sympathy for the colonial point of view and for the colonial desire for independence within the Empire than any previous Colonial Secretary. But as a man of business he also understood the economic forces behind the new imperialism of the continental powers, and he realized the responsibility of Great Britain for the economic development of her own colonial possessions, which he regarded as "an undeveloped estate".

Thus for the first time the imperial government began to take an active share in the development of the crown colonies by direct financial aid, by the building of railways and above all by subsidizing the work of tropical medicine and scientific research without which progress was impossible. These policies were fully in harmony with the older humanitarian ideals of the civilizing mission of the Empire, but they had been checked hitherto by the prevailing economic theories of *laissez faire* which discouraged any form of governmental intervention in economic matters.

Henceforward Chamberlain's ideas regarding the dual responsibility of the Empire for the welfare of the native populations and for the development of the economic resources of the dependent territories have remained the corner-stones of British imperial policy. This was not the

case, however, with regard either to the militant nationalism
of the Chamberlain period or to his more ambitious dream
of the unification of the Empire as "a federation of the
British race" based on a neo-mercantilist system of economic
self-sufficiency. For both these ideas conflicted with the
religious humanitarianism and the economic liberalism
which played such a vital part in the colonial expansion
of Britain in the nineteenth century, and this conflict of
ideas was largely responsible for the political reaction which
led to the defeat of Chamberlain and his policies in 1906.
For though the old Evangelical spirit which had been so
strong throughout the Victorian period, and which had
inspired empire-builders like Gordon and the Lawrences
and Sir George Gray, was now a declining force, liberal
humanitarianism of a more secular type was still strong and
proved far more strongly opposed to militant nationalism
and expansionist imperialism than the older religious humanitarianism, which had been profoundly conscious of Britain's
imperial responsibilities. On the other hand, the new imperialist ideology which found its literary expression in
the work of Rudyard Kipling was too crude and too aggres-
sive to win the sympathy of the great mass of middle class
opinion which had been educated in the traditions of Glad-
stonian Liberalism. It is true that Kipling's ideal of empire
was far less "jingo" and perhaps even less nationalistic
than is usually supposed. We have only to read his *Reces-
sional* to realize this.[1] Kipling's real hero is not the militarist
but the technician, the engineers and bridge-builders, the
anonymous and forgotten servants of civilization. This is
sufficiently evident in *The White Man's Burden* itself, which
is concerned not with the British Empire at all, but with
the work of the United States in the Philippines:

[1] E Halévy describes it as "une grave méditation sur la fragilité des
empires". *Histoire du Peuple Anglais,* Epilogue I, 38.

"Take up the White Man's Burden
No tawdry rule of kings,
But toil of serf and sweeper
The tale of common things.
The 'ports ye shall not enter,
The roads ye shall not tread,
Go make them with your living,
And mark them with your dead."

Nevertheless the popular misconception of Kipling's ideals is itself a sign of the misgivings that the new imperialism aroused. Nor was this unjustified, in so far as it was the expression of a new form of mercantilism which regarded the Empire primarily as a source of dividends and involved the same dangers of economic exploitation as the old mercantilism had done. Chamberlain's conception of the Empire as "an undeveloped estate" was undoubtedly liable to be abused in this sense, and so was the system of concessionary Chartered Companies. Fortunately the men on the spot usually had a higher sense of their moral responsibilities to the native population than the politicians, and it was in the service of these Companies that the new generation of imperial administrators, like Lord Lugard, served their apprenticeship.

Viewed as a whole, the imperialist movement of the '90s shows a strange mixture of the most diverse elements —of romantic idealism and crass materialism, of far-sighted statesmanship and short-sighted profit-seeking. Yet in spite of all its defects, and in spite of its failure to realize Chamberlain's full programme of imperial federation and economic self-sufficiency, it undoubtedly marks a turning-point in the relations between Great Britain and the Empire, above all in the case of the self-governing colonies, which were now well on their way towards the attainment of independent nationhood.

It created a new imperial consciousness and a new sense of imperial solidarity which prepared the way for the rise of a third British Empire, as distinct from the second Empire of the nineteenth century as the latter had been from the first Empire, which came to an end with the American Revolution. This new Empire achieved its constitutional form at the Imperial Conference of 1917, which asserted "the full recognition of the Dominions as autonomous nations of an Imperial Commonwealth and of India as an important portion of the same", a principle which was finally embodied in the Statute of Westminster in 1931. At first sight this principle was irreconcilable with all the traditional ideas of empire and imperial sovereignty, and therefore implied the creation of a new type of political organism unlike anything that had previously existed. This was recognized by General Smuts, who was one of the chief architects of the new system, in the speech to the Houses of Parliament which he delivered after the Imperial Conference of 1917. He said, "I think the very expression Empire is misleading, because it makes people think that we are one community to which the word 'Empire' can be appropriately applied. Germany is an Empire. Rome was an Empire. India is an Empire. But we are a system of nations. We are not a State but a community of states and nations. We are far greater than any Empire that has ever existed, and by using this ancient expression we really disguise the main fact that our whole position is different, and that we are not one State or nation or Empire, but a whole world by ourselves, consisting of many nations, of many states and of all sorts of communities, under one flag."

One may disagree with Smuts' terminology, but he was certainly right in his general view of the character of the British "Empire" in its final form. It was a pluralist society of a wider and more elastic kind than anything that had hitherto existed. It was at once a hierarchy of societies and a federation of federations in which peoples of all kinds could develop free institutions and national self-consciousness while preserving a common citizenship and common systems of law and mutual defence. The strength of this system is that it provides a political framework within which communities of every stage of culture and political development can co-exist peacefully and progressively develop representative institutions, until they attain the full status of autonomous nationhood. Its weakness is that it inevitably lacks the single mind and will which enabled the military empires of the past and the totalitarian states of to-day to concentrate their forces on a single object. I have already quoted Burke's dictum, "The British state is without question that which pursues the greatest variety of ends, and is the least disposed to sacrifice any of them to another or to the whole." And this is even more true of the British Empire and Commonwealth as compared with the Soviet State and Empire than it was of the first British Empire as compared with the Jacobin dictatorship. Yet in spite of this weakness, the British Empire in each of its phases has withstood the shock of war more successfully than its rivals, the military empires, which were at once more rigid and more fragile.

But can it continue to survive in the changed conditions of an age when Europe is no longer the centre of world civilization and when Great Britain herself has lost both her naval control of the seas and her economic control of the world market? Is it not inevitable and desirable that the British Commonwealth of United Nations (as Sir Robert Borden called it) should fade away and be absorbed by the completely international organization of the United Nations? But if this were to happen, it would not mean the end of imperialism, it would simply mean that the only experiment in liberal imperialism, the one Empire which had found the way to transform its provinces and dependencies into self-governing communities and ultimately into free nations, had been replaced by a much harsher and more ruthless type of imperialism, which is more concerned with the power of the strong than with the rights and interests of the weak. For although the age of European expansion has ended, the economic and scientific forces which it generated continue to operate, drawing the world closer together and increasing the pressure of the more highly organized states on the more backward peoples and the more undeveloped territories. Thus the danger of colonial exploitation remains, though it may pass under different names, and there is still a need for some power to regulate the process of development and to stand between the weaker peoples and their exploiters.

In the new world of totalitarian mass powers and intensified racial and national animosities the British Empire does represent an element of moderation and sanity which the world needs more than ever before. But it cannot perform this function if it is merely a static system of historical traditions and constitutional forms like the Holy Roman Empire. It can only justify its existence if it is the vehicle of dynamic spiritual forces. In the nineteenth century the humanitarian idealism of the Evangelical Christianity which inspired the crusade against slavery and gave the Victorians their sense of world mission and world responsibility provided this driving force. But to-day the decline of religious faith has been followed by the decline of liberal idealism, so that the British, like the rest of the peoples of Western Europe, are left with a depressing inheritance of lost hopes and deflated idealisms. Can the new democracies beyond the seas bring new spiritual forces to the aid of Western culture? For it is only in this way that the conception of the Commonwealth as an organic association of free peoples can be justified. The bond of common interest is not enough to maintain the unity of such a vast and complex organism. It also requires the bond of a common purpose which is strong enough to transcend the divergent forces of economic interest and national and racial sentiment. In the present predicament of Western culture the need of such a common purpose is evident, but it is as yet too soon to say whether the widening of the British Empire into a world-wide association of free peoples will promote the development of such a common purpose or whether the common mind and common will of the imperial society will gradually be lost in a chaos of conflicting national interests.

CHAPTER IX

Europe Overseas: the New World of America

O F all the achievements of the European expansion overseas, the creation of the United States is undoubtedly the greatest. The more the importance of Europe as the centre of world power and economic organization has declined, the more that of the United States has increased, until to-day the existence of Western Europe is becoming increasingly dependent on the economic and military power of the United States. Yet America is not only essential to the existence of Europe, it is also an essential part of Western civilization without which the survival of the latter is hardly conceivable. But though it forms part of Western civilization it is not a part of Europe, and endless misunderstandings have been caused by a failure to observe this distinction.

For the civilization of the United States has a dual character. On the one hand, it is a Western extension of European culture—on the other, it is the civilization of a New World: a world which is highly conscious of its individuality, and which feels itself to be separate and different from the Old World—not only from the world of Asia, but from the world of Europe and of Western Europe too. This dual character is deeply rooted in American history: indeed it may almost be described as the root of American history.

At first sight the English colonization of North America seems even more narrowly confined to the extension of a European national economy than the Spanish conquest of

Mexico and South America, which was inspired by crusading and missionary ideals; for the English plantations in America were primarily commercial ventures, financed and controlled by joint stock companies of the same type as the Levant Company and the East India Company. Yet almost from the beginning this unpromising development was captured and transferred by the revolutionary religious forces which were emerging in seventeenth-century England. The first settlement in New England was made by a small group of Puritan idealists, led by William Brewster and William Bradford and financed by a small company in which they had acquired shares. But before they landed at Plymouth on the shores of Massachusetts Bay, they signed a covenant which was a true social contract, constituting themselves "a civil body politic" and promising their obedience to the just and equal laws that shall be thought meet and convenient for the general good of the colony.

This compact was conceived merely as a practical application or extension of the idea of the Church Covenant which was a typical feature of the Puritan movement—"a visible Covenant, Agreement or Consent whereby men give themselves unto the Lord for the observing of the ordinances of Christ together in the same society". Nevertheless it was the germ of American democracy and the starting point of an entirely new type of colonial development. It is true that the settlement of New England was mainly due not to the little group of Pilgrims at Plymouth but to the much larger and more wealthy colony which was established ten years later at Salem and Boston. This was the work of a new Chartered Company—the Massachusetts Bay Company—like the Virginia Company and so many others. But it differed from all previous capitalist ventures of this kind in that the chief shareholders themselves took part in the migration and brought their charter with them to New England.

In this way the colony was transferred from a capitalist speculation into a self-governing community and the way was clear for an independent American development.

It is true that the Massachusetts Bay colony was far less democratic in spirit and government than the earlier Plymouth settlement, but it was no less dominated by Puritan religious ideals and it came to accept the same Congregational and covenanting principles of ecclesiastical policy and the same identification of the Church with the political community. These principles inspired the whole development of society in New England. They were embodied above all in the system of town government which originated with the Plymouth settlers and became characteristic of New England as a whole. The town, or as we should say the township, was the primary social unit: and it found its constituent principle in the local Church and the Church covenant. Thus Church, school and town meeting were all organs of one spiritual community which exercised a strict control over the moral and economic life of its members.

This democratic theocracy with its intensive moral discipline and its strong communal spirit was the creative force behind the development of New England. No doubt it was narrow, intolerant and repressive and it excluded a large part of the population from Church membership and full civic rights. Nevertheless the Congregational ideal was fundamentally democratic, and the basing of citizenship on membership of the Church and Church membership on personal conviction gave the whole social system a unitary character which it could never have derived from purely political institutions. It meant that the social order was not an external one imposed on the individual by authority and tradition, but a spiritual partnership which involved personal responsibility and a consciousness of spiritual privilege.

The result was that from the first the New Englanders felt themselves to be a chosen people and were entirely free from the sense of inferiority which has often marked early colonial societies. They believed, in the words of one of their leaders,[1] that "God had sifted a whole nation that He might send choice grain over into this wilderness"; while another of the early settlers[2] wrote "Know this is the place where the Lord will create a new Heaven and a new Earth in new Churches and a new Commonwealth together".

There was nothing in the external conditions of New England life to justify utopian hopes. The early colonists had a hard struggle to maintain their existence in a harsh environment from an ungrateful soil. But these external conditions combined with the rigorous spiritual discipline of Puritanism to create a new society of a remarkably homogeneous type, which possessed its own culture and its own social and moral ideals.

Conditions in the Southern colonies, and above all in Virginia, were entirely different from those in New England and produced a correspondingly different type of society. The economic life of Virginia was based on the cultivation of tobacco, which involved considerable capital and a plentiful supply of labour. Thus the primary social unit was the individual plantation, worked by negro slaves or semi-servile indentured servants, in contrast to the township of New England with its communal economy and its Congregational policy. Thus though there was little difference in social origin between the original settlers in the two regions, economic conditions in the South favoured social inequality and produced a social cleavage between the wealthy slave-owning planters of the Tidewater districts and the independent farmers of the uplands and the pioneer settlers of the

---

[1] William Stoughton, c. 1630–1701.
[2] Edward Johnson, c. 1599–1672.

back country. At the same time the contrast between Virginia and New England was increased by the fact that the South was officially Anglican in religion and possessed much closer economic and cultural relations with England.

The difference in social structure between the two groups of colonies was so great that it might even be maintained that it was greater than the difference between either of them and the society of the mother country. But this divergence of social type was largely overcome by the development of the Middle Colonies which formed a transitional zone and acted as a bond of union between North and South.

The oldest of these was Maryland, founded in 1634 by a Catholic, Lord Baltimore, who hoped to attract English Catholic settlers. Thus while it closely resembled Virginia in its economic and social structure, it differed both from Virginia and New England in its religious tradition, since it was the first of the American colonies to establish the principle of religious toleration by the Toleration Act of 1649. The same principle inspired the foundation of the colonies of Providence and Rhode Island in 1636 and 1644 by Roger Williams, who went further than any man of his time in demanding absolute unconditional freedom of conscience, even to the "permission of the most Paganish, Jewish, or anti-Christian consciences and worships." As Maryland belonged to the South, so Rhode Island belonged to New England by its social structure, but it was founded as a deliberate protest against the authoritarian exclusiveness of the New England theocracy. It was moreover remarkably democratic in its form of government, so that in several respects Rhode Island anticipated the later development of American society and of the American way of life.

The typical Middle Colonies of New York and Pennsylvania were of later foundation. In fact, it was not until the eighteenth century that their key position in the development of America became manifest. But even from the first these colonies were distinguished alike from Virginia and from New England by the mixed character of their population and their links with continental Europe. In New York the Dutch element long retained its importance and produced a stable, wealthy society which resembled that of Virginia in its large estates and in its employment of negro slaves, although it also possessed an important mercantile element which was ultimately to make the city of New York a great commercial and financial power.

The second great Middle Colony, Pennsylvania, resembled New England in that it owed its origin to a spirit of religious idealism. Penn founded his colony as a Christian state in which the Quaker ideals of toleration and brotherly love might be realized. But it was not intended to be an exclusively Quaker society. From the beginning it was a land of refuge for the persecuted minorities of the Christian world, and Penn encouraged the immigration of refugees of all denominations—Mennonites and Schwenkfeldians, Protestants from the Palatinate, French Huguenots, Welsh Dissenters and Ulster Presbyterians. Thus Pennsylvania became a melting pot of nationalities and religions and inaugurated the new era of European migration which eventually had such a vast influence on the course of American development.[1]

This was the more important because Pennsylvania was the chief gateway to the interior, through which the movement of colonization passed westward towards the Ohio and southwards into the Valley of Virginia. In these regions a new society grew up, remote from the influences of Europe and the old settled society of the Eastern coast. It was a

[1] A somewhat similar policy was adopted in the first half of the eighteenth century by the founder of Georgia, General Oglethorpe, but unfavourable economic conditions stunted its development.

semi-barbaric society without towns or schools or churches, carrying on a ceaseless war with the forest and the Indians. But it was a new world free from all the restrictions of government and privilege and possessing unlimited land and opportunity for expansion. This frontier society was not peculiar to the Middle Colonies, though they played an exceptionally important part in its development, owing to their geographical position. But it was to be found in all the colonies from Georgia to New York and New Hampshire which had access to the interior, and in all of them it produced a common way of life and a common social type. This new way of life and this social type were more distinctively American than anything that existed in the old colonial society, and it was here that the colonists first turned their backs on Europe and embarked on the new task of the conquest of a continent by the axe and the rifle.

Thus the frontier played a vital part in the movement for American independence. It was during the long struggle with the French and the Indians for the conquest of the Northwest Territory that the colonies first became conscious of their common interests in the development of the continent and that men like Washington served their apprenticeship in war and came to know the West and its possibilities. And in the same way the closing of the conquered territories to colonial settlement by Great Britain in order to avoid conflict with the Indians was one of the chief causes of the hostility of the colonists to imperial centralization and European control.

It was, however, not on the frontier but in the seaport towns of New England, above all at Boston, that the American Revolution originated. As we have seen, New England possessed from the beginning a strong tradition of independence which was rooted in its religious origins and in the democratic and contractual tendencies of the Congregational policy. "We came hither," wrote Cotton Mather in 1702, "because we would have our posterity settled under the full and pure dispensation of the Gospel; defended by rulers that shall be of ourselves." It is true that Mather was no democrat, but there were others, like the Rev. John Wise (1652–1725), who did not shrink from the extreme conclusion that "power is originally in the people", that all men are by nature free and equal, and that "Democracy is Christ's government in Church and State".[1] Thus New England possessed an inherited bias towards republican and democratic ideas, and when the movement against the Stamp Act and the excise duties started, it was easy for the commercial interests affected to appeal to the instinctive hostility of the common people against an alien and unpopular authority.

The chief organs of this popular agitation were the secret societies known as "The Sons of Liberty", which were mainly responsible for the outbreak of rioting in the seaport towns of Massachusetts and Connecticut in 1765 and for the reign of intimidation and mob law that followed. But this outbreak of revolutionary violence would have had no permanent success without the help of the dominant elements in colonial society—the merchants and lawyers of New England and the aristocratic land-owners of Virginia. And the alliance of these extremely disparate elements would have been impossible unless they had found a common ideology which could unify their various interests and ambitions. It was the existence of this common doctrine which transformed the American revolution from a petty squabble about colonial taxation into a crusade for the rights of man which changed the course of history. As Thomas Paine wrote fifteen years later: "What we

[1] *Vindication of the Government of the New England Churches.*

formerly called Revolutions were little more than a change of persons or an alteration of local circumstances. They rose and fell like things of course, and had nothing in their existence or their fate that could influence beyond the spot that produced them. But what we now see in the world, from the Revolutions of America and France, are a renovation of the natural order of things, a system of principles as universal as truth and the existence of man, and combining moral with political happiness and national prosperity.""[1]

The elements of this doctrine were not new. They were the old principles of natural law and the social contract derived from Locke and Blackstone and Burlamaqui and the Puritan divines. Had not John Cotton, one of the fathers of New England, declared that "it is evident by the light of nature that all civil relations are founded in Covenant. For to pass by natural relations between Parents and Children and violent Relations between Conquerors and Captives; there is no other way given whereby a people (sui Juris), free from natural and compulsory engagements, can be united and combined together into one visible body""[2]? But hitherto no one had attempted to make these ideas the foundation of a new state, and when Thomas Jefferson framed the Declaration of Independence, the assertion of the "self-evident truths" of the Rights of Man and the nature of government was accepted by public opinion as a new gospel of liberation and hope. But even before the Declaration had been made, the full ideological implications of the conflict had been clearly expressed by Thomas Paine, the obscure English exciseman who did even more than the New England agitators or the Virginian statesmen to win the emotional support of the American people for the new

[1] Thomas Paine, *The Rights of Man*, p. 135. (Everyman Ed.)
[2] John Cotton, *The Way of the Churches in New England* (1645).

ideology. In his famous pamphlet *Common Sense*, he sweeps the legal and constitutional issues impatiently aside and appeals in flaming rhetoric for the liberation of mankind and the creation of a new world. "O ye that love mankind . . . ," he writes, "stand forth; every spot of the old world is overcome with oppression. Freedom has been hunted round the globe. Asia, Africa have long expelled her. Europe regards her like a stranger and England has given her warning to depart. O! receive the fugitive and prepare in time an asylum for mankind. . . . We have it in our power to begin the world over again. A situation similar to the present hath not happened since the days of Noah until now. The birthday of a new world is at hand, and a race of men perhaps as numerous as all Europe contains are to receive their portion of freedom from the event of a few months. The Reflection is awful—and in this point how trifling, how ridiculous do the little paltry cavillings of a few weak or interested men appear, when weighed against the business of a world."[1]

As in all revolutions, there was a wide gap between revolutionary ideology and revolutionary politics, but the case of America differs from that of seventeenth-century England or eighteenth-century France in that it was a new country and a new world, so that the exalted hopes of the revolutionary idealists were matched by the vast resources of an unexploited continent and the unlimited possibilities of social expansion. In eighteenth-century France Thomas Jefferson might have been a constitution-monger like Sieyès, or more probably he would have gone to the guillotine with the Girondins. In America he was able not only to take a leading share in the formation of American political thought, but also to play an effective part as a practical politician in the government and development of his country.

[1] T. Paine, *Common Sense*, pp. 58–9 (1776).

For his conception of democracy as a free commonwealth of freeholders liberated from the economic and political servitudes of the Old World and free to exploit the inexhaustible resources of a new continent was not a utopian dream. It was a practical policy which could appeal alike to the Virginian planter, the Pennsylvanian democrat and the frontiersman. Moreover, Jefferson not only formulated the republican policy, he also realized the conditions for its fulfilment by his purchase of Louisiana, which assured the agrarian expansion of the United States, if not, as he believed, "to the 100th and 1,000th generation", at least for the next hundred years.

Finally, Jefferson gave classical expression to the theory of foreign policy which underlies not only the Monroe Doctrine but also the whole tradition of American isolationism. This new "American system" of foreign policy was in his view the necessary international corollary of the Declaration of Independence, which must "point the course which we are to steer through the ocean of time opening on us". As he wrote to Monroe in 1823, "I have ever deemed it fundamental for the United States never to take active part in the quarrels of Europe. Their political interests are entirely distinct from ours. Their mutual jealousies, their balance of power, their complicated alliances, their forms and principles of government are foreign to us. They are nations of eternal war. All their energies are expended in the destruction of the labour, property, and lives of their people. On our part, never had a people so favourable a chance of trying the opposite system of peace and fraternity with mankind, and the direction of all our means and faculties to the purposes of improvement instead of destruction".[1] Therefore "our first and fundamental maxim should be never to entangle ourselves in the broils

[1] Letter to the President, June 11, 1823.

of Europe. Our second, never to suffer Europe to inter-
meddle with cis-Atlantic affairs".[1]

The early years of the Republic were especially favourable to the growth of these isolationist ideals, for during
the greater part of the first four presidencies—from Washington to Madison—the Old World was absorbed in the wars
of the Revolution and the Empire, and communications were
reduced to a minimum by the Embargo and the Continental
Blockade. Everything during these impressionable years,
culminating in the war of 1812, the burning of Washington
and the ruin of the trade of New England, was calculated
to strengthen the aversion of Americans from the Old World
and their belief in the independent destinies of their continent. For during the same period, the West was being
opened to settlement, and the new states of Kentucky, Ten-
nessee, Ohio and Louisiana had been founded, while in the
six years after the peace six more states—Indiana, Missis-
sippi, Illinois, Alabama, Maine and Missouri—were added
in rapid succession. The creation of these ten new states
entirely changed the balance of power in the federation and
made the influence of the frontier a dominant factor in
American politics. These new states differed from the thirteen
original states by their lack of the historical roots and traditional state patriotism, so that they were more national in
character, while their comparative poverty and absence of
class feeling rendered them far more democratic both socially
and politically than the Eastern states.

This new element first achieved political power with the
election of Andrew Jackson as President in 1828. Jackson
was in every respect the living embodiment of Western
prejudices and Western ideals. He was a frontiersman of
Ulster stock, a self-made man who had grown up with
the new West and was its champion in politics and war,

[1] Letter to the President, October 24, 1823.

a mortal enemy of the Indians, and the man who defea
the British Army at New Orleans. His election meant
advent of a new type of American democracy equally rem
from the middle-class Puritanism of New England and
patrician idealism of Jefferson. This was the new n
democracy which made such a deep impression on
Tocqueville in 1831. He saw more clearly than any of
contemporaries the tremendous elemental power of the for
which were at work in the new society. In his eyes "
gradual and continuous progress of the European r
onwards towards the Rocky Mountains had the solemn
of a providential event. It [was] like a human delu
rising unabatedly and driven daily onwards by the hand
God".

When de Tocqueville wrote, the great Atlantic migrat
had hardly started. The first settlement of the West v
predominantly American, and the newcomers from Eur
were largely English farmers like the members of Birkbec
agricultural colony in Illinois, or social and religious ideal
like Owen's settlers at New Harmony.

But in the '40s the movement changed its charac
Political discontent and economic hardship set in mot
an immense wave of popular migration from Germany a
Ireland. However, this vast influx of European populat
did nothing to strengthen the bonds between Europe a
America but rather had the opposite effect. For the n
comers fled to America as a refuge from famine and politi
oppression, and tended to look back with aversion to Euro
Thus the great migration of the '40s and '50s reinforced
original revolutionary myth of Europe as the unnatu
mother and England as the harsh and tyrannical fat
from whom the innocent children had escaped to find a r
home in the New World. As Paine had written in *Comm
Sense:* "Europe and not England is the parent country

America. This new world hath been the asylum for the persecuted lovers of civil and religious liberty from every part of Europe. Hither have they fled not from the tender embraces of the mother but from the cruelty of the monster."[1]

Nevertheless, though the new European immigration had its place in the American social pattern and contributed to the development of American ideals, it tended to weaken the homogeneity of Anglo-American society. The newcomers had not received the training in self-government which was part of the colonial heritage. They possessed different religious and political traditions, and a different attitude to the state. And consequently their coming gradually produced changes in political technique, above all in party organization and in town life and government, which were to have an increasing influence on American institutions during the second half of the nineteenth century.

This influence was increased by the fact that a large part of the new population, and especially the Irish, settled in dense masses in the cities of the north-east, where they provided an abundant supply of cheap labour for the new American industrialism. The advent of this new industrialism was no less revolutionary in its effects on American society than it had been in Europe. It is true that it was less highly concentrated than it had been in England, owing to the size of the country, and the continual expansion of agricultural settlement kept pace with the advance of urban industrialism. Yet on the other hand, the rapidity of the change from the primitive conditions of the frontier to the most advanced type of industrial development was more violent than anything known in Europe, while the importance of the agrarian element in American political traditions, as represented by Jeffersonian republicanism and Jacksonian democracy, had

[1] Op. cit., p. 45.

no real analogy in Europe. No doubt there was in England
a sharp conflict between the industrialists and the old landed
interest which came to a head in the controversy on the
Corn Laws and the victory of Free Trade. But in America
the conflict was both wider and deeper. It involved fundamental constitutional and moral issues like the question of
state rights and the institution of slavery, and it divided
state against state and the society and culture of the North
against those of the South. The resultant war marks the end
of the old American tradition and the beginning of a new
order. The war left the South economically ruined and
politically insignificant, so that the balance between the
agrarian South and the commercial North was destroyed
and the historic political partnership of Virginia and New
England in the leadership of the Republic came to an end.
It was fortunate for America that the North was led throughout the struggle by one of the greatest representatives of
American ideals. Nevertheless the Northern victory did not
mean the victory of Lincoln's spirit or of Lincoln's ideals,
for the post-war period was marked by a general slump in
ideals, and the leadership of America passed from the statesmen to the men of business. It was the age of the great
financiers and captains of industry, men like Jay Gould and
William H. Vanderbilt, John D. Rockefeller and Andrew
Carnegie and Philip Armour, Jay Cooke and J. Pierpont
Morgan.

These were the men who reaped the fruits of the Civil
War and directed the vast movement of material expansion
which took place during the last three decades of the nineteenth century. These men wielded a power which was un-
dreamed of by the founders of the Constitution. They were
economic imperialists who created new empires of gold and
steel and oil. But they were also representative Americans
who did more to determine the evolution of modern Ameri-

can civilization than either the thinkers or the politicians. And their influence was the greater because they were working in a new social environment and with new human material. For the tide of immigration which had set in during the middle of the century was now flooding the East and the Middle West, so that the new cities and the new industries were being filled by a new population drawn in increasing proportions from the overpopulated areas of Southern and Eastern Europe—especially Italy, Poland and Galicia.

This dual interrelated process of capitalist expansion and European immigration produced important changes in the class structure of American society. In the South there had been an aristocracy of planters and a proletariat of "poor whites" and negro slaves, but the West, and especially the frontier region, had been remarkable for its social uniformity. Now, however, there was an aristocracy of financial and industrial magnates and a proletariat of wage-earners who spoke a different tongue and belonged to a different race from their masters. It is true that the new society was politically democratic, at least in theory, but the social inequality between a Rockefeller and a Polish worker was greater than that between a Southern planter and the poorest of white share-croppers. Thus the new industrial order not only produced an immense increase of national wealth and power, it also increased social tensions and class conflicts which often expressed themselves with extraordinary violence and bitterness, as in the Homestead Strike at Pittsburgh in 1892 and the Pullman Strike at Chicago in 1894. It is not surprising that it was an age of disillusionment for the writers and thinkers who represented the old social traditions and the old spiritual ideals. Their disillusionment is expressed no less clearly, though in very different terms, by Henry Adams, the representative of the highest cultural traditions of New England and old America, than by Mark Twain, who represented the popular democratic tradition of the West from the age before the Civil War.

But perhaps the most remarkable example of this change of attitude is to be found in the work of Herman Melville, who stands midway between these younger writers and the great New England writers who belong to the age before the Civil War. In his early period, no writer surpassed Melville in his professions of faith in the American ideal, which he conceives in definitely Messianic terms. "We Americans," he writes, "are the peculiar chosen people— the Israel of our time; we bear the ark of the liberties of the world. Seventy years ago we escaped from thrall; and besides our first birthright—embracing one continent of earth—God has given to us for a future inheritance, the broad domains of the political pagans, that shall yet come and lie down under the shade of our ark, without bloody hands being lifted. God has predestinated, man expects great things from our race, and great things we feel in our souls. The rest of the nations must soon be in our rear. We are the pioneers of the world, the advance guard sent on through the wilderness of untried things to break a new path in the New World that is ours."[1]

A quarter of a century later, in *Clarel,* this optimism has vanished and Messianic hope has changed to apocalyptic despair:

> "Behold her whom the panders crown
> Harlot on horseback riding down
> The very Ephesians who acclaim
> This great Diana of ill fame!
> Arch strumpet of an impious age,
> Upstart from ranker villeinage,

[1] *White-Jacket,* Ch. XXXVI (1850).

'Tis well she must restriction taste,
  Nor lay the world's broad manor waste:
  Asia shall stop her at the least
  That old inertness of the East."[1]

"But in the New World things make haste
  Not only things, the *state* lives fast
  Fast breed the pregnant eggs and shells,
  The slumberous combustibles,
  Sure to explode. 'Twill come, 'twill come!
  One demagogue may trouble much:
  How if a hundred thousand such?
  And universal suffrage lent
  To back them with brute element
  Overwhelming? What can bind these seas
  Of rival sharp communities
  Unchristianized? Yes, but 'twill come!"

"Indeed these germs one now may view:
  Myriads playing pigmy parts,—
  Debased into equality:
  In glut of all material arts
  A civic barbarism maybe:
  Dead level of rank commonplace:
  An Anglo-Saxon China, see
  May on your vast plains shame the race
  In the Dark Ages of Democracy."[2]

It was not long after Melville wrote these lines that the
transformation of America by urbanization, foreign immigration and the empire of big business was completed. Yet
even when that transformation was almost complete in the

---

[1] *Clarel* by Herman Melville, Vol. II, p. 240.
[2] Ibid., Vol. II, pp. 249–50.

last decade of the nineteenth century, the vitality of the old American ideals and social traditions showed itself in the revolt of the Western agrarian Populists led by Bryan against the domination and capitulation of the party machine. The defeat of the Populists by McKinley and Mark Hanna seemed to mark the triumph of the new order dominated by Wall Street and based on the exploitation of alien labour. But it was a transitory victory, and the coming of Theodore Roosevelt at the beginning of the new century marks the turn of the tide.

Roosevelt was important not so much for what he did as for what he said—for his policies rather than his achievements. He realized that "the total absence of governmental control" had led to a greater concentration of economic power in the hands of the few than existed in any other country, and he proclaimed the necessity of breaking the power of the trusts and reasserting the authority of the executive alike over financial interests and over the party machine. He recognized the justice of the Populist complaint of the exploitation of the agrarian West by the financial powers of the East,[1] and he saw that under the new conditions the American tradition could only be maintained by abandonment of the principle of *laissez faire* and the adoption of a positive policy of social and economic reform.

Roosevelt, like Bryan, was broken by the party machine, but his defeat involved the victory of the Democrats. And the Democrats under Wilson in 1913–21, and still more under the younger Roosevelt in 1933–45, did more than Theodore Roosevelt himself could have done to realize his demand for a new policy of social reform. At the same time,

---

[1] But he saw farther than Bryan. More than any man in his time he realized that the real problem was not the exploitation of the farmers by the financiers but the exploitation of nature by man and the rapid exhaustion of the natural resources of America by a ruthless demand for quick and easy profits.

by a historical accident it fell to the Democrats to lead America into both the great World Wars, a task for which they were less suited by history and tradition than the Republicans, who from the time of McKinley and Theodore Roosevelt had been the representatives of an active foreign policy and had stood for the realistic acceptance of America's position as a world power. Now, however, the Democrats, who were the natural representatives of the Jeffersonian tradition, were forced by the accident of political power to assume responsibility for American participation in European wars and European peace settlements, while the Republicans became the spokesmen of the traditional American attitude of isolation and detachment from "the ferocious and sanguinary conflicts of Europe".

The result of this reversal of roles has been to complicate the already intricate relations between America and Europe. The fact that it was the idealist party that accepted the burden of intervention and the responsibility for internal order has accentuated the idealistic elements in American foreign policy, while the fact that it was the realist party which rejected the League of Nations has accentuated the realistic elements in the policy of isolationism. This element was conspicuously absent from the original isolationist ideology, and President Coolidge's dictum "The business of America is business", is far more remote from the Jeffersonian ideals than President Wilson's appeal for a new world order based on the principle of justice to all peoples and all nationalities.

But in 1920 the issue of isolation was still a living one, since there was still a European system from which it was possible to withdraw. After 1945 this was no longer the case. The old European society of states has been destroyed. The Atlantic is no wider than the English Channel was a century ago, and America finds herself forced to play the leading role in a world which is rapidly growing smaller. The same ideals which formerly caused America to turn her back on the Old World in order to build a new society based on natural rights now impel her to assert the same principles in international politics and to become the architect of world order and the defender of Western civilization.

But although Americans still accept these ideals as part of their social inheritance and as the spiritual foundations of their political constitution, they no longer have the same meaning and social content as they had in the past. For the fifty years between the Civil War and the First World War had changed the American way of life even more drastically than the age of the Revolution had done. Washington and Jefferson and Lincoln are extinct social types which belong to an American past that is just as remote as the past of Europe. The old freedoms of the New England farmer and the Virginian planter and the Western frontiersman are not the freedoms of the Common Man of to-day, the citizens of Megalopolis and Middletown and Main Street. In the past both the American problems and their political and social solutions were essentially different from those of the Old World. To-day they are essentially the same. Alike in America and Europe, Western civilization is faced with the problem of how to reconcile the old spiritual values with the new techniques of mass civilization and mass power. This underlying similarity is temporarily concealed by the fact that the technical leadership of American civilization, which was achieved during the later nineteenth century, has enabled it to preserve the institutions and also the illusions of nineteenth-century liberalism[1] more successfully than Europe,

[1] The word "liberal" is used in a somewhat different sense in America to that which is current in Europe. In the European sense of the word the American Revolution was a "liberal" movement and Franklin and Jefferson were typical "liberals". But in America they have been so canonised by national tradition that their liberalism has acquired the character of a conservative orthodoxy.

which was exposed to the full blast of the anti-liberal reaction. But this is only a transitory phenomenon, and the
two great provinces of Western civilization are merely passing through different stages of the same process. We should
remember that it was in America that de Tocqueville was
first led to his great discovery of the totalitarian tendency
inherent in mass civilization and of the new dangers to
human freedom that lay hidden in democratic institutions.

   "I had remarked," he writes, "during my stay in the
United States that a democratic state of society similar to
that of the Americans, might offer singular facilities for
the establishment of despotism, and I perceived upon my
return to Europe how much use had already been made
by most of our rulers of the notions, the sentiments and
the wants engendered by this same social condition, for
the purpose of extending the circle of their power. This
led me to think that the nations of Christendom would
perhaps eventually undergo some form of oppression like
that which hung over several nations of the ancient world.
A more accurate examination of the subject, and five
years of further meditations, have not diminished my
apprehensions but they have changed the object of them.
. . . I think [now] that the species of oppression by which
democratic nations are menaced is unlike anything which
ever before existed in the world: the old words despotism
and tyranny are inappropriate: the thing itself is new;
and since I cannot name it, I must attempt to define it.
   "I seek to trace the novel features under which despotism may appear in the world. The first thing that
strikes the observation is an innumerable multitude of
men, all equal and alike, incessantly endeavouring to
procure the petty and paltry pleasures with which they
glut their lives. . . . Above this race of men stands an

immense and tutelary power, which takes upon itself alone to secure their gratifications and to watch over their fate. That power is absolute, minute, regular, provident and mild . . . it would be like the authority of a parent, if like that authority its object was to prepare men for manhood; but it seeks, on the contrary, to keep them in perpetual childhood. . . . For their happiness such a government willingly labours, but it chooses to be the sole agent and only arbiter of that happiness; it provides for their security, foresees and supplies their necessities, facilitates their pleasures, manages their principal concerns, directs their industry, regulates the descent of property and subdivides their inheritance. What remains but to spare them all the care of thinking and all the trouble of living? Thus it every day renders the exercise of the free agency of man less useful and less frequent; it circumscribes the will within a narrower range and gradually robs a man of all the uses of himself. The principle of equality has prepared men for these things; it has predisposed men to endure them and often to look upon them as benefits."[1]

The last hundred years have realized all de Tocqueville's predictions; indeed the reality has often gone far beyond anything that he foretold. It is true that the loss of freedom and the trend to totalitarianism have gone further in Europe than in America, but this also is in accordance with de Tocqueville's prediction. For it was his thesis that the United States, which were the original home of equalitarian principles, were protected from their full consequences by a series of factors which mitigated the tyranny of the majority. In the first place, they had inherited the tradition of personal freedom from their colonial ancestors together with the tradition of local self-government. In the second place,

[1] *Democracy in America*, Vol. II, part iii, Ch. 6, translated by Henry Reeve.

this tradition was a religious one, so that "Americans combine the notions of Christianity and liberty so intimately in their minds that it is impossible to make them conceive of one without the other", and even the sovereignty of the people and the absolute right of the majority were held to be subject to the binding principles of the Christian moral law. In the third place, the fundamental laws and Constitution of the United States had been expressly framed to protect liberty by the separation of powers and the federal form of government which was intended to prevent the establishment of a centralized state. Finally, the unlimited land and resources of a virgin continent were a safeguard against the social tensions and economic conflicts which were the great causes of despotism in the Old World.

To-day none of these factors remains intact; the Civil War, the filling-up of the continent and the change in the composition of the population have made the United States a different social organism to that which de Tocqueville knew. Yet for all that, the existence of these traditions and the part that they played in the formation of modern American society have saved the United States from totalitarianism and from the full political and economic consequences of the equalitarian principle. Nevertheless, though the process has been slowed down, it has not been stopped. A society cannot continue to live indefinitely on the traditions of a vanished social order. In some respects the techniques of modern mass civilization are more advanced in America than they are in Europe, and they are bound to exert a growing influence on politics unless they are controlled by some positive spiritual force and guided by positive rational principles. In the past American society derived this force from the religious idealism of sectarian Protestantism, and its principles from the eighteenth-century ideology of Natural Rights and rational Enlightenment. But to-day both these forces have lost their power. American religion has lost its supernatural faith and American philosophy has lost its rational certitude. What survives is a vague moral idealism and a vague rational optimism, neither of which is strong enough to stand against the inhuman and irrational forces of destruction that have been let loose in the modern world. Here America is faced by just the same problem which confronts Europe, which is the problem of Western civilization as a whole. In both cases an age of unparalleled economic expansion and material prosperity has been accompanied by a neglect and loss of the spiritual resources on which the inner strength of a civilization depends. The danger is more acute in Europe than in America because the process of disintegration has gone farther and the revolt of the irrational forces in culture has been more open and more destructive. Yet the situation is no less serious in America than in Europe, because American society has given itself up more wholeheartedly to the processes of material expansion and spiritual extroversion and has been less aware of the inherent instability of the age of progress and of the nature of the spiritual forces which threaten the destruction of Western culture.

Thus on neither side of the Atlantic is there any room for self-complacency and self-congratulation, or any advantage to be gained by maintaining the old controversies and criticisms and the old claims to moral and cultural superiority which were characteristic of the last century. Western civilization cannot be saved either by Europe or by America; it demands a common effort which cannot be limited to immediate political ends, but must involve a deeper process of co-operation based on common spiritual principles. It has been the strength of the American tradition that it was consciously founded on these principles as represented by the eighteenth-century ideology of Natural

Law and human rights. The great problem to-day is how these principles can be re-established on foundations which are both spiritually deeper and sociologically more realistic than the rational constructions of eighteenth-century philosophy.

PART II

THE PRESENT CRISIS OF WESTERN CULTURE

CHAPTER X

Intellectual Antecedents: Hegel and the German Ideology

THE situation in which we find ourselves involved to-day is an extraordinarily complex one. The world is passing through a process of violent change, accelerated by war and revolution, the effects of which are felt even in the most remote and backward societies of Asia and Africa. But it is in Europe that this movement of change originated and it is from Europe that it has been propagated, so that it is only by understanding Europe that we can understand what is happening to the world.

Unfortunately the crisis has become so much a part of our daily lives and affects the conditions of our material and social existence so immediately that we are obliged to take action whether we understand the nature of the crisis or no. And, since the primary responsibility for action falls upon the politicians, it is they and not the philosophers who have to explain to the ordinary man what is happening and what he has to hope and fear in this changing and catastrophic world. Now we cannot expect the politicians to look very deep into the past or very far into the future. Their answers must be simple, easy and optimistic, otherwise they could not expect to gain majorities or to win support for their party politics.

Nevertheless it is not the politicians who are primarily responsible for the crisis. The scientists and the technicians, the philosophers and the theologians and the men of letters have played a larger part than the politicians themselves in

producing those great changes of culture which have transformed the modern world and ultimately led to the present
world crisis. In the preceding chapters we have seen how
the making of Europe and the successive changes of
Western culture are mainly the result of spiritual and
intellectual forces which are not political in origin though
they have their consequences on the political plane. The
average man is at least dimly aware of the existence of such
movements as Christianity, the Reformation, the Enlightenment and the French Revolution, modern science and
technology, Liberalism, Socialism and Communism—though
he is not fully aware how deeply they have entered into the
substance of his life and thought. What we all tend to
forget, however, is the way in which even the most irrational
phenomena in the modern world, such as nationalism,
racialism and totalitarianism have been conditioned and in
some cases created by the philosophies and ideologies of
the past, so that behind the modern demagogue and dictator
there stands the ghost of some forgotten metaphysician.
This point is so important and so underestimated that I
think it is worth while to take the case of one of the most
influential philosophers of the past before we attempt to
analyse the nature of the present crisis.

This philosopher is Hegel, who stands as it were at the
cross-roads of the nineteenth century. It is not merely that
his thought has helped to form the German political ideology
and the German idea of the state. He stands for much more
than that. Indeed his is one of the most seminal minds of
the nineteenth century. He stands behind Karl Marx and
the modern Communist ideology. He inspired the Russian
revolutionary intelligentsia before and after Marx. He had
a great influence on Fascism, especially on the rationalization of the Fascist state by Gentile. Alone among modern
works, his *Philosophy of Right* has had an equal influence

on the conservatives and the revolutionaries and there is hardly a political movement in modern times that has not been affected by it in some measure. Yet in spite of his international importance, he remains profoundly and characteristically German, and it is not surprising that many thinkers have looked on him as the source of the ideas which have had such a devastating effect on European civilization during the last thirty years. "In the bombing of London," wrote Professor Hobhouse during the last war, "I had just witnessed the visible and tangible outcome of a false and wicked doctrine the foundations of which lay, I believe, in the book before me"—Hegel's *Philosophy of Right.*

But if the *Philosophy of Right* is the quintessence of Prussianism, how is it that it should have had so powerful an influence on Communism and Liberalism, while National Socialism itself, which by universal agreement is the incarnation of the forces of evil in the German tradition, should have ignored it? In Rosenberg's *Myth of the Twentieth Century* there are only a couple of references to Hegel, both of them hostile, compared with seventeen references to Kant and a whole chapter devoted to Schopenhauer; whereas in Ruggiero's *History of European Liberalism,* it is Hegel and the disciples of Hegel who occupy the centre of the stage. At first sight this is very surprising when we read the bitter attack on German Liberalism which prefaces the *Philosophy of Right,* but if we read it more closely we find that the Liberalism which Hegel attacks has a much closer affinity to National Socialism than to Hegel's own doctrine. It is the Liberalism of the first German Youth Movement, of the Wartburg Party Rally and the emotional appeal to the spirit of the German *Volk* and *Land.* It is even possible to see a certain parallelism between the cult of political violence, as shown in the murder of Kotzebue and the attempted murder of Ibell, and the attitude of National Socialism to the assassins of Erzeberger and to Horst Wessel. Against all this Hegel protests in the name of reason and law.

"The special mark which it carries on its brow," he writes, "is the hatred of law. Right and ethics and the actual world of justice and ethical life are understood through thoughts; through thoughts they are invested with a rational form, i.e. with universality and determinacy. This form is law; and this it is'which the feeling which stipulates for its own whim, the conscience that places right in subjective conviction, has reason to regard as its chief foe. The formal character of the right as a duty and a law it feels as the letter, cold and dead, as a shackle; for it does not recognize itself in the law and so does not recognize itself as free there, because law is the reason of the thing and reason does not allow feeling to warm itself at its own private hearth. Hence law, as I have remarked elsewhere in the course of this book, is *par excellence* the shibboleth which marks out the false friends and comrades of what they call 'the People'."[1]

All this applies to National Socialism as well as to the Liberal Populism which was Hegel's enemy, and he was equally unsparing in his denunciation of the anti-rational traditionalism of von Haller, who was adopted as the official political philosopher of German Romanticism. Hence it is difficult to see in a Hegel a Nazi or the father of Nazism.[2]

[1] *Philosophy of Right*, trans. T. M. Knox, Preface, p. 7. (Oxford, 1942.)
[2] It must be admitted, however, that Hegel at times comes very close to modern German neo-Paganism in his religious views: e.g. the passage published by Rosenkranz in the appendices to his *Life of Hegel* (p. 552) in which the latter advocates the encouragement and organization of the peasant custom of the Midsummer Fire as a popular festival. "This joy in the Fire needs only to be taken in earnest," he says, "in order to become a divine service. But it is not taken in this way. Man, in the Religion of Suffering, despises his joy and rejects the consciousness of it."

But when we come to the question of "Prussianism", the case is different. It is true that Hegel was not himself a Prussian and in his early writings he writes of Prussia with the antipathy that was so common among Germans at that time. But this was before the great changes that made the Prussian state the intellectual leader of Germany; and from the time that he went to Berlin and found in Altenstein, the Minister of Education, not merely a patron but a disciple, he became the devoted servant of the Hohenzollern monarchy and one of the spiritual fathers of the new Prussia.

There was indeed a kind of elective affinity between the Prussian state and the Hegelian philosophy. For the Prussian people, unlike any other people in Europe, had been made by the state and for the state, by a conscious process of military and political organization. For centuries the slow stubborn squires and peasants of North-Eastern Germany had been hammered and drilled into a new shape by the will of their rulers and the brains of their officials. Nor, as we have already seen, were the latter necessarily Prussians. The men who contributed most to the creation of the new Prussia in the nineteenth century were of the most diverse origins. Hardenburg was a Hanoverian, like Scharnhorst; Stein was from Nassau; Gneisenau was a Saxon and had fought in the English service in America; while in the eighteenth century some of the foremost servants of the Prussian state, like Lucchesini, de Launay, and Suarez were not even Germans.

Such a state was made to appeal to Hegel, who of all the philosophers of his generation—and indeed of all modern philosophers—had the strongest sense of the state and who realized most deeply the importance of the power factor in history and politics. If history is the process of the self-manifestation of spirit, if it is the business of philosophy not to construct an ideal republic, but to comprehend the

real world and the state as the centre of it, then the state
which is most conscious of itself as a state, and least inclined
to subordinate itself to, or merge itself in, civil society will
be the best state. "If the state is confused with civil society,"
writes Hegel, "and if its specific end is laid down as the
security and protection of property and personal freedom,
then the interest of the individuals as such becomes the
ultimate end of their association and it follows that the
membership of the state is something optional. But the
state's relation to the individual is something quite different
from this. Since the state is mind (*Geist*) objectified, it is
only as one of its members that the individual himself has
objectivity, genuine individuality, and an ethical life."[1]

In writing thus Hegel was setting himself in conscious
opposition to the strongest currents of contemporary thought;
not only to the rising tide of European Liberalism but to the
rational individualism of Kant and the eighteenth-century
Enlightenment. In England, above all, both philosophy and
politics tended to the exaltation of the rights of the individual and the security of property and limitation of the
powers of the state. Civil society was everything and the
state was its instrument and servant. But in Hegel we
already find the beginning of that degradation of terms
which has transformed the classical "civil society" into
"bourgeois society" and the "citizen" of the First French
Republic into the "bourgeois" of Communist ideology.
From the first he had stressed the economic character of
civil society as a "Society of Needs" and had tended to
regard the bourgeois as the sub-political type, the man who
withdraws himself from the ethical totality of the state to
serve the limited interests of his family and his class. Left
to itself economic society becomes a blind chaos in which
all the higher values are sacrificed. Man's needs are capable

[1] Op. cit., p. 156.

of indefinite expansion, and as wealth increases society becomes more inorganic, because wealth loses its relation to labour. "The bestiality of the contempt for all that is high supervenes. The volume of wealth is the motive, and the absolute bond of the people, which is the ethical element, disappears and the people is lost."[1] Therefore the state must intervene to control this blind unconscious impulse by a corporative organization which defines the social obligations and functions of the economic and industrial society. "The sanctity of marriage and the dignity of Corporation membership are the two fixed points around which the unorganized atoms of civil society revolve."[2]

Now it is important to remember that this dualism of a "*bürgerliche Gesellschaft*" without political responsibility and devoted to economic activity, and a hierarchic bureaucratic state, which stands above and apart from the citizen body, is not the arbitrary creation of Hegel's political theory. It corresponds to the political realities of Hegel's age and country. While in England "civil society" was a politically conscious community which embraced all men of property and at the same time played an active part in the government of the country, in Germany the conditions were still almost mediaeval. The *Bürger* was not only a member of a caste and a corporation, he was strictly a burgess, that is to say his citizenship was not that of a nation but of a city which in many cases was actually a city-state. Hence for a German the expression "*bürgerliche Gesellschaft*" held a totally different social content from that of the English "civil society", of which it was supposed to be a literal translation. The inhabitant of the German Imperial Cities, which were still so numerous when Hegel was a young man, was a member of a little separate world segregated from the

---

[1] *Das System der Sittlichkeit* (*Werke*, vii., 496).
[2] *Philosophy of Right*, p. 154 (§ 255).

life of the state in the modern sense, and the pettiness of interest which such conditions generated is reflected in the term *Spiessbürger*, "petty bourgeois", which Karl Marx uses so frequently and with so much contempt. Above this little world there was the world of the princes and their courtiers and officials, the world of Baroque palaces and *Residenzstädte*. And beyond that again was the remote and archaic pomp of the Holy Empire with its Diets and its Aulic councillors, a venerable ghost the memory of which still shadowed the court of Vienna and the councils of the Germanic Confederation.

Now in order to create a living political society out of this archaeological museum, Hegel looked not to the bourgeoisie, who seemed to him the most deeply sunk in selfish particularism, but to his own class,[1] the officials and the professors who seemed to him the class which by its very nature was dedicated to the service of the whole, "the universal class". And since Prussia was the typical *Beamtenstaat,* a state of officials and officers in which the king himself was a glorified civil-servant-by-divine-right, it was right and proper that Hegel should find in Prussia his spiritual home, and the field in which to sow his ideas.

Nevertheless his idea of the state had little in common with the cold-hearted calculation of Frederick the Great and his pupils. In his view the state is never a mere political instrument, it "must be treated as a great architectonic structure, as a hieroglyph of the reason which reveals itself in actuality".[2] "We should desire to have in the state nothing except what is an expression of rationality. The state is the world which mind (*Geist*) has made for itself; its march, therefore, is on lines that are fixed and absolute. How often we talk of the wisdom of God in nature! But we are not

---

[1] Hegel's father was an official in the Würtemberg fiscal service.
[2] Op. cit., p. 228.

to assume for that reason that the physical world of nature is a loftier thing than the world of mind. As high as mind stands over nature, so high does the state stand over physical life. Man must therefore venerate the state as the Divine upon Earth (*das Irdisch-Göttliches*) and observe that if it is difficult to comprehend nature, it is infinitely harder to understand the state."[1] "The March of God in the world, that is what the state is."[2]

If this is rationalism, it is not the rationalism of the rationalists, and it is derived from very different sources from those of the Prussian tradition of statecraft. Behind the Hegel of the *Rechtsphilosophie* there is the youth who had once shared with Hölderlin the intoxicating vision of Hyperion—the true city in which man is one with the gods, where the finite and the infinite are united in the totality of a living community.[3] How far apart their paths had led since those early days! Hölderlin following his vision, like Eurydice, down to the dark underworld of insanity, Hegel never relinquishing his hold on reality until he had subdued it by the sheer force of thought and incorporated it with all its contradictions in the totality of an absolute synthesis. The turning point in Hegel's thought seems to have taken place in 1802–3, at the same time as Hölderlin's tragedy. It was then that Hegel first gave clear expression (in his pamphlet on the Constitution of Germany) to all those elements in his thought that we regard as characteristically Prussian: power politics, an anti-democratic conception of government, Machiavellianism, above all the exaltation of war as a necessary and health-giving law of existence.

[1] Op. cit., p. 285.
[2] Op. cit., p. 279.
[3] This concept of *"Totality"*, which originates with Schiller, was of decisive importance in the intellectual development alike of Hegel, Hölderlin and Schelling, and through them the idea of the total community became part of the Romantic tradition.

But in the circumstances of the time in which Hegel wrote all these ideas were not so much Prussian as Napoleonic. It was the hour of Napoleon's triumph and of Germany's humiliation: not the humiliation of national defeat as in the years of Austerlitz and Jena, but the humiliation of internal disintegration when the German princes were fawning on the First Consul for their share in the spoils of confiscated Church lands and the débris of the Holy Empire. In those days Bonaparte rose above the satraps of Germany like a new Alexander, and it was in him and not in the Hohenzollerns or the Hapsburgs that Hegel found the pattern of his "world-historical individual" in whom the movement of history is embodied and who transcends law and morality by his creative activity.

These ideas were by no means specifically Prussian or German. They were in the mind of an age which had witnessed the French Revolution and had seen the dramatic succession of leaders—Mirabeau, Danton, Robespierre, Hoche, Moreau, Bonaparte—rising and being swept away in turn by the forces that they had embodied or created.

"These are the living instruments of what is in substance the deed of the world mind and therefore they are directly at one with that deed though it is concealed from them and is not their aim and object. For the deeds of the world mind, therefore, they receive no honour or thanks either from their contemporaries or from public opinion in later ages."[1]

"If we go on to cast a look at the fate of these World-Historical persons, whose vocation it was to be the agents of the World Spirit—we shall find it to have been no happy one. They attained no calm enjoyment; their whole life was labour and trouble; their whole nature was nought

[1] *Philosophy of Right*, p. 218.

else but their master passion. When their object is attained, they fall off like empty husks from the kernel. They die early, like Alexander; they are murdered, like Caesar; transported to St. Helena, like Napoleon. . . .

"It is in the light of their common elements which constitute the interest and passions of individuals that these historical men are to be regarded. They are *great* men, because they willed and accomplished something great; not a mere fancy, a mere intention, but that which met the case and fell in with the needs of the age. . . .

"A World-Historical individual is not so unwise as to indulge a variety of wishes to divide his regards. He is devoted to the One Aim, regardless of all else. It is even possible that such men may treat other great, even sacred, interests inconsiderately; conduct which is indeed obnoxious to moral reprehension. But so mighty a force must trample down many an innocent flower—crush to pieces many an object in its path."[1]

These are the words of the philosopher. Now hear the words of the man of action, Billaud Varennes, member of the Committee of Public Safety:

"The decisions for which we have been reproached we did not wish for the most part two days, a day or several hours before taking them. It was the crisis alone that produced them. In this sphere of tempests we could only see the common safety; we made a dictatorship without giving it any other name. *Dictatorship* we said in a voice that Europe could not drown. It was a dictatorship, a revolutionary government that led by violence to the Republic. We were *statesmen*; putting the safety of the cause entrusted to us above every other consideration.

[1] *Philosophy of History* (Sibree's translation), pp. 32–4.

Do you reproach us with the means we used? But the means made that great cause to triumph. Our eyes were fixed too high to see that the ground on which we trod was covered with blood. Reproach us if you will but also say: 'They did not fail the Republic.' "

And if we turn to the greatest writer in the opposite camp —to Joseph de Maistre—we find not indeed Machiavellianism, but the same sombre conception of historic destiny and the immanent force of events as well as a far stronger justification of war and the sacrifice of the innocent than anything that Hegel wrote.[1] After all, a generation which had experienced twenty-three years of almost continual war was bound to give war a considerable place in its system of thought, and men who had seen Europe turned upside down and European society transformed by the power of the sword were all more or less believers in power politics. It is not in this that Hegel's originality is to be found, but rather in the stubborn determination with which he maintained his faith in the rationality of history and of the state as the perfect embodiment of spirit—the actuality of the ethical idea. He had deepened the eighteenth-century conception of law and politics by his profound consciousness of the concrete reality of social change and the dialectical movement of history. He saw the state not as a political mechanism, but as a moral organism by membership of which alone man can achieve freedom and full moral activity. Man only acquires rights as member of a social system, and this system is not a juridical abstraction but a concrete living historical organism. History is a process of the construction of such organized systems which are at once systems of institutions and systems of minds, and thus

[1] E.g. the chapter, "*De la destruction violente de l'espèce humaine*", in his earliest work. *Considérations sur la France*, and the Seventh Conversation in the *Soirées de St. Petersbourg* on the divinity of war.

it is a second world, a spiritual creation which can be compared to the world of nature in its diversity and organic interrelation, while it transcends that world by its universal consciousness and its actuality of concrete freedom and ethical order.

Now, according to Hegel, it is in the state that this process of organization culminates. It is the all-embracing organization, self-contained, self-conscious, self-determined: an autonomous totality, a complete moral world, the ultimate fruit of the tree of life, the "Divine Idea as it exists on earth". Thus Hegel lays the metaphysical foundations for that cult of the state which has become to an increasing extent the religion of the modern world. It is strange that a man who possessed such a deep and rich sense of history should not have realized that this attribution of absolute and ultimate value to a particular social form limits the movement of history and impoverishes its spiritual values. For it is only in the ancient oriental civilizations, which Hegel terms the first world-historical realm, that the state is a spiritual totality. Elsewhere culture transcends the state not merely ideally but sociologically, so that it is only in a society of states that the cultural whole is to be found. Even the city-state of ancient Greece, which was the source and pattern of Hegel's conception of the state as an ethical totality, was in reality itself a member of a wider society, and it was this society, this Pan-Hellenic world, which was the true Whole in which the spirit of Hellenic culture found expression. And this was still more true of Western civilization, all the typical achievements of which transcended the limits of the state and depended on the fruitful interaction and co-operation of the different European peoples.

Moreover, behind this European community there lies in fact the historical reality of Christendom, the commonwealth of Christian peoples, which did not derive its origin from the state, but was on the contrary the spiritual basis which the European state assumed as given and from which its highest values were derived. Hegel's extremely limited view of the nature of religion and the function of the Church made it impossible for him to do justice to these facts. Hegel always declared that he was a Lutheran and he was in fact in his later years a loyal adherent to the official conception of the Prussian State Church as exemplified in Altenstein's ecclesiastical policy. But it was a very residual and negative Lutheranism in which the Church had become no more than a docile and sentimental *Hausfrau* of a state which itself embodied the spiritual principle in a masculine and objective form.

Hegel was a true Protestant in the sense that he protested with passion and conviction against a Church which claimed to be the objective embodiment of the Spirit and the representative of the transcendent majesty of Divine Law. But he was no less opposed to the sectarian Protestantism which turned men's minds from the state and from the present world and absorbed them in personal piety. It is characteristic of Hegel's "Lutheranism" that he found "the hero of Protestantism" not in Gustavus Adolphus or Cromwell, but in Frederick the Great, the man who "had the consciousness of Universality, which is the profoundest depth to which Spirit can attain". What Hegel valued in the Reformation was in fact that it had destroyed the Church as a substantial unity and had restored the unity of human consciousness in one universal objective moral organism—the state. For Hegel's real religion is the Religion of the State: a hybrid growth which owes its external features to the official Lutheranism of the territorial churches of the German principalities, but which derives its true inspiration from the ideal of the Greek city-state, where, as he remarks, the name of the city "suggests not only a complex of political institutions

but no less that Goddess who represented the spirit of the
people and its unity".

To the last, Hegel's glorification of the state as the embodiment of the divine idea—as "this actual God"—retains the
traces of the Platonic idealism of his romantic youth when,
with Schelling and Hölderlin, he attempted to recapture a
lost spiritual world of infinite reality and beauty. But this
vision of perfection (like the vision of Blake and Wordsworth
and Shelley in England) had no earthly relation with the
actual conditions of the modern state, and the *tour de force*
by which Hegel identified the two is a typical example of
that irrational leap in the dark from Spirit to Nature and
from Logic to Reality with is the Hegelian idea. The fact
is that Hegel's conception of *Geist* or Spirit is profoundly
equivocal and covers an infinite gradation of meanings.
When the Romantics at the close of the eighteenth century
spoke of Spirit, they were using a word that was charged
with immense weight of Christian tradition and mystical
depth. And this is no less true of Hegel, who began as a
theologian and remained in a sense a theologian to the end.
But his identification of Spirit with rational activity—not
only the creative activity of the cosmic Logos but also, and
no less, the rational activity of the human mind objectifying
itself in law and institutions—introduced another element
into the conception, which deprived it of its transcendent
character and opened the way for the complete secularization of both the concept and the system by the Hegelians
of the Left, culminating in Feuerbach and Marx.

Now the conception of a society which should be the
earthly embodiment of the Spirit—a Spirit-created and a
Spirit-filled organism—was no invention of the Romantics:
it was a common possession of the whole Christian past.
Indeed this society was the spiritual home of European man
to a greater degree than the state, and not least in Germany

where the territorial state possessed only the bare bones of political authority and military power without the organic life of a true civil society. Consequently when Hegel transfers to the state by a *coup d'esprit* the rights and prerogatives of the spiritual community and arrays the grim skeleton of the police state in the royal robe of Divinity, he is not only denying the Christian doctrine of a supernatural order and a super-political society; he is not even doing justice to the social ideals of the Romantics in which he had once shared. The words which Hölderlin's Hyperion addresses to his friend Alabanda before their parting are a prophetic criticism of the false path his friend was to follow, to the misfortune of Germany and of Europe.

"You grant the State yet too much power," he says. "It should not demand what it cannot compel. For the gift of Love and of the Spirit cannot be forced. Let it leave them untouched, or let men take its law and nail it to the pillory. By Heaven he knows not how he sins, who would make the State a moral schoolmaster. Whenever man has sought to make the State his Heaven, he has made it Hell.

"The State is the coarse husk round the fruit of life and nothing more. It is the wall round the garden of human fruit and blossom.

"But of what use is the wall round the garden when the earth lies dry and barren? Only the rain from heaven can help.

"O rain from heaven, O breath of the Spirit, Thou wilt restore to us the springtime of the peoples.

"The State has no jurisdiction over thee. But if it does not hinder thee, thou wilt yet come, thou wilt come with thine almighty glory and raise us above mortality."[1]

[1] Hölderlin, *Werke* (Insel Ausgabe), p. 456.

This eschatological vision of the descent of "the youngest, fairest daughter of time, the new Church", is almost identical with the vision of the renewal of Christendom with which Novalis concluded his *Europa,* while at the same time in England William Blake was creating a similar apocalypse on a gigantic scale in the series of epics which culminated in *Jerusalem.* The descent from these cloudy summits of the romantic Sinai to the worship of the Secular State, that Golden Calf in the desert of materialism, is one of the strangest events in the history of European thought, and the philosophy of Hegel remains as a mighty monument and symbol of this spiritual journey into the wilderness.

CHAPTER XI

The Revolt Against Europe

THE change in the world position of European culture during the present century has been so great that it is difficult to find any parallel to it in the whole course of history. In comparison with this the greatest changes in the history of ancient civilization, like the decline of Hellenistic civilization in the second century B.C. or the decline of the Roman Empire in the fourth and fifth centuries A.D., were comparatively gradual and were far more limited in their effects. Fifty years ago Europe enjoyed a position of world hegemony which was at once political, economic and cultural, which had been steadily growing for four centuries and which showed little apparent sign of coming to an end. In the course of little more than a single generation this position of world leadership has been lost and Europe herself is threatened with disintegration. Politically, Europe to-day is weaker and more divided than at any period since the tenth century. Fifty years ago her political and military powers were greater than those of all the rest of the world put together, and she was the centre of control in which all the forces of international politics were concentrated. To-day the centres of world power lie outside Europe, and Europe herself is partitioned between two rival non-European power systems. From the economic point of view her productive resources are still great, but she has become relatively and absolutely impoverished, and she has ceased to be the workshop of the world and the centre of world trade and finance.

Even more serious than all this, however, is Europe's loss of cultural leadership. In the past Europe has undergone many political and economic crises, some of them very severe, like that which caused the ruin of Germany during the Thirty Years' War, but hitherto no one in Europe and few outside have doubted the values of European culture. To-day all this has changed. Asia and Africa are in revolt, not merely against the political control of Europe, but even more against her claim to cultural hegemony. America is convinced of her own cultural superiority, as represented by what is known as "the American way of life", and is coming to regard Europe as a culturally backward area which stands in need not only of American money but of American methods of social organization and American cultural leadership.

Finally and above all, Europe herself has begun to lose faith in her own cultural traditions and her own cultural values. The external critics of European culture find supporters within European society. Indeed these critics have been the disciples of the internal critics of the European tradition, so that to a very great extent Europe has been her own greatest enemy.

This is something new in history. In the second century B.C. Hellenism was the victim of an anti-Hellenic reaction, but no Greek and few men of Hellenistic culture ever doubted the supreme value of the Hellenic tradition. And so, too, in the decline of Rome, the prestige of Roman culture outlasted the power of the Empire. There were traitors and renegades who went over to the barbarians for practical reasons, but there was no anti-Roman ideology, and men remained faithful to the old tradition of culture for centuries after the political order had broken down. No doubt the change from paganism to Christianity involved a revolt against cultural tradition and a change of cultural values, but this was an internal process within Mediterranean culture, and the transfer of loyalties had already taken place and a new synthesis had been created before the fall of the Empire.

This double movement of criticism and disaffection towards the social traditions and cultural values of our civilization is therefore a unique phenomenon in history. It is not a result of political decline, since it preceded the latter and developed during the century when the external power of Europe was at its highest. On the contrary, it may be argued that it was this revolt against European culture that was one of the antecedent causes of Europe's political decline, since the anti-European ideologies have provided the enemies and rivals of Europe with their most formidable weapons, while the internal loss of faith in European culture has weakened the European powers of resistance in external political and economic relations.

Consequently the crisis of European culture is not merely of interest to the historian and the philosopher, it must be a vital concern to the statesman: indeed it is a matter of life and death to every part of the European community and to every citizen of Europe. Nevertheless it is not possible to understand it without going deep into questions which lie beneath the surface of history and which are far outside the ordinary range of political discussion.

In the first place, it is necessary to understand the unique character of the European development. As I have shown in the third chapter, Europe has always differed from the other world cultures in its non-unitary nature. The contrast is most obvious in the case of China, which is a state, and in a sense a nation, as well as a civilization. But it may be said that all the oriental world cultures aspire to a monolithic unitary form—a form which achieved its most perfect expression more than four thousand years ago in ancient Egypt[1] and which recurs again and again in the successive world empires of the oriental world.

Europe, on the other hand, has never possessed this kind of unity. She has been a society of peoples, united by a common spiritual tradition. Her existence depends on the maintenance of a delicate balance between the centrifugal force of nationality and the common spiritual traditions which make for unity. The co-existence of these different forces and the maintenance of a balance between them is an essential condition of the European achievement and the source of the richness and many-sidedness of European life. But it also means that European culture is more *labile*— more exposed to the danger of social and spiritual disintegration—than are the older and simpler forms of oriental culture. For in the case of Europe the unitary principle is neither geographical nor racial nor political, it is a spiritual principle which has been superimposed on the underlying diversity of many different peoples and cultures that have been drawn together by a common faith into a new spiritual community with common moral values and common intellectual culture.

In its origins this community was a religious one. Europe was Christendom and the Catholic Church was the bond and organ of European unity. Nevertheless the loss of religious unity which took place four centuries ago did not destroy European unity. For at the same time that the unity of Christendom was lost, the unity of Europe was reinforced on the intellectual plane by the influence of Renaissance culture. During the last four centuries the humanist tradition has been the great bond of European unity. The Catholic and Protestant peoples have shared the same discipline of classical education and have ac-

[1] Perhaps an even more remarkable example is the prehistoric civilization of the Indus valley, which shows no sign of any change or development during all the centuries of its existence.

cepted the same cultural standards and values. Nor was this tradition merely a literary and intellectual one. It was as a creator of moral values that humanism exercised its greatest influence on the European way of life and thought. The Hellenic tradition of ethical idealism flowered anew in sixteenth- and seventeenth-century Europe and bore fruit in a new conception of human personality and in a moral criticism of life which was more profound than that of classical antiquity because it was enriched by a thousand years of Christian experience.

Thus in spite of the loss of Christian unity and the growing independence of the national state, the flowering of Western culture in the sixteenth and seventeenth centuries possessed an international Pan-European character, owing to the influence of the humanist tradition. We see this not only in the new art, the new drama and the new philosophy of the Western peoples, but also in the new mathematical science and the new knowledge and control of nature. Galileo and Bacon, Huyghens and Leibniz and Newton belong just as much to the humanist tradition as do the classical scholars. In spite of the religious wars and the political rivalries which seemed to tear Europe asunder, science and art knew no frontiers, and the republic of letters was a cultural unity which transcended political and national divisions.

Thus there was no question of an "iron curtain" in seventeenth-century Europe, for even the ideological division between Catholics and Protestants did not seriously interfere with the transmission of culture, as we see from the immense popularity that a Jesuit moralist like Baltasar Gracián enjoyed even in Protestant Europe.

Nevertheless the dualism of religion and culture which was latent in the humanist culture of these centuries did involve a potential danger to European unity. This became obvious in the eighteenth century when the philosophers of the Enlightenment attempted to complete the work of the humanists by creating an autonomous humanist culture which should be independent of religion and tradition. Thus the relative values of Christian humanism were transferred into absolute ends, and the abstract ideal of "civilization" took the place of the historic tradition of European culture. In the same way the humanist criticism of life which had found creative expression in the classical writers of the humanist period, like Cervantes and Shakespeare, was replaced by a rationalist criticism of the beliefs and institutions of the Christian and European past. It is true that the leaders of the movement, like Voltaire, were in a sense good Europeans who were highly conscious of the unique achievements of European culture. But at the same time nothing was safe from their destructive criticism. They used the abstract concepts of Reason and Truth and Civilization as weapons to attack every truth and to undermine the foundations on which the actual historic structure of European culture rested. Thus in the centre of Western Europe, in the midst of one of the most sophisticated and highly cultural societies that the world has known, there arose a movement which denied the eternal truths of Christianity and the moral values of humanism and the historical achievements of European culture. Men even began to ask whether civilization itself was not a gigantic mistake and whether it was not possible for humanity to shake off the burden of history and tradition and to rebuild society anew on natural foundations.

The full implications of this movement were not revealed for more than a century, since even the French Revolution was only a preliminary and partial manifestation of the new forces. There was an inherent contradiction between the naïve rationalism of the Enlightenment which initiated the movement and the irrational instinctive forces which it liberated. For though the latter showed themselves clearly enough in the Terror and in figures like Marat and Hébert, they were not strong enough to overcome the rational and authoritarian elements which were so deeply rooted in the French tradition and which reasserted themselves more strongly than ever during the Consulate and the Empire in the person and work of Napoleon. The real meaning of the Revolution is to be seen perhaps more clearly in its enemies than in its supporters. The rising of the peoples against Napoleon was the starting point of the modern nationalist movement which has had an even more dissolvent effect on the European tradition than the French Revolution itself. Fichte, who was the great ideologist of this nationalist movement, was himself a disciple of the French Revolution, which had inspired his early writings. But his boundless subjectivism and individualism led him by devious paths to the idealization of the state as the creator of freedom and the sole organ of economic life and social culture, and finally culminated in a deification of the German people as "the one race in whom the germ of human perfectibility is most decisively present and to whom the progress of its development has been entrusted".

But though Fichte was the ideologist of the German revolution, he was a transitional figure who still had his roots in the eighteenth century. The deeper implications of the movement were more fully realized in his younger romantic contemporaries, above all in the life and work of Heinrich von Kleist. Kleist was a patriot and a leader in the national awakening, but his great poetic dramas like *Penthesilea* and the *Hermannschacht* are not inspired by Fichte's idealization of the national genius but by a negative ecstasy of destruction, a kind of death-mysticism which found its final expression in his dramatic suicide on the shores of the

Wannsee in 1811. Here at last the implications of the revolutionary movement are no longer concealed by a veil of utopian idealism; they are revealed in their true nature, as an opening of the gates of the abyss and a liberation of the dark irrational forces which had been chained by a thousand years of Christian culture.

Throughout the first half of the nineteenth century Germany continued to be the workshop of revolutionary ideas which were all the more revolutionary because they were purely theoretical and found no outlet in revolutionary action. This work was carried on simultaneously on three different planes—by philosophers like Schopenhauer and Feuerbach and Stirner, by men of letters like Buchner and the Young German writers, and by the Socialists like Bruno Bauer, and Moses Herz and Karl Marx. The latter are almost forgotten to-day with the exception of Marx, who owed a great deal to his immediate predecessors but who repaid his debt, as was his habit, by boundless ridicule and invective.

It was from this three-fold source that the European revolutionary movement penetrated Russia and found there a fertile soil for further development. In Russia even less than in Germany was there any outlet for the expression of revolutionary thought in political action, so that the whole movement was forced underground, and helped to increase the cleavage in Russian society and culture which was already so strong. Ever since the end of the seventeenth century Russia had been undergoing a process of Westernization which found its external embodiment in the new Western capital of St. Petersburg and which throughout the eighteenth century continued to transform the organization of the Russian state and the culture of the ruling classes. This revolution from above was inevitably unpopular, since it was in conflict with the whole spirit of the East Slavonic-

Byzantine traditions of Muscovite Russia, and it aroused a stubborn, inarticulate resistance which found expression in Cossack risings, peasant unrest and the religious protest of the Old Believers and the other schismatic sects.

But from the second quarter of the nineteenth century onwards, this native tradition of opposition itself became transformed by the infiltration of Western revolutionary ideas. The ideologies of the German philosophers and the French and German Socialists were transplanted to Russia and acquired a more revolutionary character in the new environment. Thus Western ideas no longer formed a bond between Russia and the West, but acted as an explosive force which widened the gap between them. Even a conservative and traditional movement like that of the Slavophils, which derived its inspiration from the German idealization of race and nationality, helped to strengthen the revolutionary forces by its hostility to the work of Peter the Great and its return to the traditional ideal of Holy Russia. All these different currents mingled with one another in the closed world of the Russian intelligentsia to produce the Russian revolutionary tradition. Unlike the contemporary revolutionary movements of the West it was not primarily political, but cultural and religious. It was in fact a kind of negative religion which preached the gospel of atheism and materialism with the same uncompromising fanaticism which had characterized the Russian sectarian movements.

This spirit found its extreme manifestation in Nihilism, that peculiarly Russian phenomenon which arose in the '60s under the influence of Bakunin and received its intellectual formulation from writers like Pisarev, Chernishevsky and Dobrolyubov.

Its significance has been well described by Nicholas Berdyaev in the following passage:

"Nihilism is the negative of Russian apocalyptic. It is a revolt against the injustices of history, against false civilization; it is a demand that history shall come to an end, and a new life, outside and above history, begin. Nihilism is a demand for nakedness, for the stripping from oneself of all the trappings of culture, for the annihilation of all historical traditions, for the setting free of the natural man, upon whom there will no longer be fetters of any sort. The intellectual asceticism of Nihilism found expression in materialism; any more subtle philosophy was condemned as a sin."[1]

The influence of Nihilism is far greater than that of the group of writers who first popularized its doctrines. It permeates the whole revolutionary tradition in Russia and was particularly strong in the case of P. N. Tkachev, the first great leader of Russian Marxism. And though it is underestimated or ignored by the official historians of Communism, it was undoubtedly one of the most important factors that contributed to the breakdown of the old régime and the victory of the November Revolution.

I have spoken of the Russian revolutionary movement at some length, not only on account of its intrinsic importance as the source of the greatest existing world challenge to European culture, but still more because it is the classical example of the process by which European revolutionary ideas can be assimilated by non-European cultures so that they become transformed into anti-European ideas. What happened in Russia in the last century is happening to-day in Asia and is about to happen in Africa. And in every case we see the same sequence: first cultural nationalism, then social revolution and finally the denial and rejection of the higher cultural values.

[1] *The Origin of Russian Communism,* p. 49.

All these phases are equally present in Western Europe itself. It was here that they had their origin, and from Europe they have spread like an epidemic to all parts of the world in proportion as they are open to the influence of European culture. But the effect of these forces in Europe is far more serious than elsewhere, since here they threaten the very life of our culture, whereas in the East they are relatively external to the native cultural traditions.

Thus oriental nationalism has not the same dissolvent character as it has in Europe, since it tends to unite the whole culture against foreign influence and domination. In fact the unit of oriental nationalism is not really a national one, but is the civilization itself, as in China, and to some extent also in India and Islam. Similarly, the higher cultural values that are denied are not the traditional oriental ones, but the imported values of Western civilization which have been imperfectly assimilated and have never appealed to the deeper needs of the oriental soul.

But this is far from being the case in Europe. The European nation has always been a part of the greater unity of European culture, and when in the nineteenth century nationalism made its absolute claim to spiritual and cultural autarchy it inevitably had a disintegrating effect on European unity. The effects of this were not so serious in the old Western kingdoms, where the state had possessed a national character for centuries; but in Central Europe, where the nation-state did not exist and where the rise of nationalism coincided with the rise of the revolutionary movement, the results were disastrous. The historical development and the political structure of Central Europe had been formed by the supranational tradition of the Holy Roman Empire and the multinational tradition of Hapsburg Austria. The former was destroyed by the Revolution and the latter was undermined and disintegrated by the convergent attack of

German and Slav nationalism. This had a disastrous effect on Europe as a whole, since it removed the keystone of the European order and destroyed the existing system of international co-operation which had been laboriously constructed by the leaders of the great powers at Vienna in 1814–15. But in Central Europe itself it meant much more than this, since it involved the tearing asunder of the organic unity of a living culture between rival nationalities and rival racial ideologies. It was in view of this situation that Grillparzer, as the representative of the old Austrian civilization, made the saying I have already quoted, that "the path of modern culture leads from humanity through nationality to bestiality", and the hundred years that have passed since he wrote have done nothing to weaken the force of his indictment.

As I have pointed out in Chapter IV, this nationalist disintegration of Central Europe led to a series of great European wars which ultimately destroyed the whole European state system. The multiplication of new national states increased the instability and insecurity of the new order, since each of them had to struggle at once against the external pressure of some neighbouring great power and against the internal pressure of its own national minorities. The old European order had rested on a complex of historical traditions and social relations which were to some extent the common possession of the different states and were deeply rooted in the European past. The network of diplomatic relations between the European capitals was only the formal and specialized expression of a much wider system of social relations between the ruling élites in the different countries, which formed an international society and a supranational class. This European society and class as it existed in the nineteenth century was no doubt unsatisfactory from many points of view. It was to a large extent a survival from the days of the ancient régime entrenched behind a barrier of aristocratic privilege and divorced from the life of the common people. Nevertheless it was always open to men of talent who were not of aristocratic origin, men like Guizot, Stockmar, Sir Robert Morant, the American historian J. L. Motley, Henry Reeve and the like—and its disappearance was not the result of its social exclusiveness, but rather of its tolerance and comprehensiveness, which conflicted with the growing exclusiveness of nationalist culture. Thus there was no common European democratic culture to take the place of the old aristocratic society and the disappearance of the social élites which were linked with the European whole rather than the national parts destroyed the natural organs of international communication and produced a gradual lowering of the higher standards of European culture.

Nevertheless the triumph of nationalism was less complete than it appeared at first sight. For at the very time when the nationalist states were successfully asserting their political and cultural independence, their internal cohesion was being undermined by a great movement of economic change. As the industrial revolution spread from Britain to the Continent and finally from Western to Eastern Europe, the life of both the workers and the middle classes was completely transformed and their mutual relations were radically altered. The class conflict which was the inevitable result of the process of industrial urbanization, cut across the issues of nationalism and racialism and created the new internationalisms of capital and labour.

This new situation was reflected in the Marxian ideology and propaganda, which made the class conflict the basis of social theory and political action and acted as a ferment of revolutionary change from one end of Europe to the other. Although Marxism was purely Western in origin and derived its inspiration from the realities of English industrialism, from the theories of German philosophy and from the ideals of the French revolutionary tradition, its action was felt most strongly in Eastern Europe in the lands of peasant culture where the influence of urban industrialism was most recent. It was to the uprooted peasants and the half-emancipated Jews who had lost their vital links with their old way of life in a stable peasant community or a traditional religious culture that Communism and Socialism brought a new faith and a new way of life. And since these elements had never had any share in humanist culture or any conscious loyalty to the European tradition, they had no difficulty in rejecting them as the culture and tradition of an alien ruling caste.

In the West the situation was quite different. The leaders of the English Labour movement were often more attached to humanist ideals than were their capitalist opponents, and they found their natural allies among the leaders of the romantic return to the traditions of mediaeval Christendom like Ruskin and William Morris, while in France the ideology of Proudhon, the most influential of French socialist thinkers, was the very antithesis of Marxism alike in its moral traditionalism and in its hostility to the State and to all forms of collectivism and regimentation.

It was however in the West, and especially in Great Britain, that the process of urban industrialism went furthest and detached society most completely from its natural roots in the soil. The urban society ceased to be closely related to its own country and region and became the servant of the world market and the organ of a cosmopolitan economy.

This process of urban industrialization produced an extraordinarily rapid increase of wealth and population, but at the same time it weakened the vitality and cohesion of European culture and involved the vulgarization and cheapening

of man as well as of his work. The new machine-made
civilization which Western Europe and America spread
over five continents was a cheap and ugly civilization and
it aroused the antipathy not only of the conquered cultures,
but also of considerable elements in Europe itself. Nor was
this antipathy confined to the exploited classes or the oppressed nationalities; it also affected the privileged classes
and found its strongest expression among the leaders of later
nineteenth-century culture, such as Friedrich Nietzsche. It
was Nietzsche who first clearly realized the nature of the
disease of European culture in the *Nature and History of
European Nihilism*—and the fact that he failed to provide a
cure and that his remedies were merely advanced symptoms
of the disease should not blind us to the truth and depth of
his diagnosis. Although Nietzsche was a German of the Bismarckian era and was not unaffected by the exaggerations of
contemporary German nationalism, he regarded himself first
and foremost as a "good European" who was loyal to the
great tradition of Western humanism as the source of all the
higher spiritual values of European culture. At the same
time he recognized that this humanist culture had exhausted
its energy and that the spiritual values which it had created
were being dissolved in a mush of humanitarian sentiment
and liberal idealism. Above all, the higher human types were
being absorbed and destroyed by the human herd which
swarmed in the new cities and which was being drilled
into uniformity by the democratic and bureaucratic state.

Nietzsche attributed the main responsibility for this process of degeneration to the influence of Christianity and
Christian moral teachings. Although he recognized the historic importance of Christianity as a creator of spiritual
values, he failed to realize that Christianity was no more
responsible for the degradation of European ethics than
humanism was responsible for the degradation of European

culture. Christian values and the humanist values had both alike become devaluated. Only the economic values remained, and they possessed no spiritual power and provided no common cultural aim. Science and technology had immeasurably increased the knowledge and external power of Western man only to leave him spiritually naked and empty before the abyss of Nihilism.

In Nietzsche's view this crisis could only be overcome by the discovery of a new spiritual aim which would create new values and give a new meaning to life. This aim could not be found in humanity itself. For in spite of Nietzsche's humanism he realized that Man was not an end, but the way to an end. If the old religious faith was dead, and the old philosophic and moral idealisms had become hollow abstractions, man could only escape from spiritual destruction by finding a new goal beyond humanity. Here Nietzsche was at one with the Christians whom he condemned. His thesis is essentially a religious one, and he saw far more clearly than most of his Christian contemporaries that the crisis of Western civilization was neither political nor economic but essentially spiritual—a crisis in the soul of Western man. On the other hand, his attempt to provide a solution to the problem by the gospel of the Superman and the Will to Power is even more fallacious and irreligious than any of the solutions propounded by the socialists or the secular humanitarians and had a most disastrous influence on European, and particularly on German, thought in the early twentieth century. For what is the Superman but a distorted shadow of the heroic ideal cast on the abyss by the setting sun of humanist culture? And what is Nietzsche's Will to Power but the prevalent moral disease of modern culture in an exaggerated form? No doubt there was in all this an element of delusion and megalomania which were the premonitory symptoms of his own mental disease, but to a large extent it was the logical consequence of his misunderstanding of Christianity and of the antipathy which he naturally felt for what he falsely supposed to be Christian values and ideals.

In Nietzsche's eyes Christianity was nothing but masochism and fear of life, a slave morality of submission and suffering, the revenge of the weak on the strong and of the sick on the healthy. No doubt there was much in contemporary Christianity to excuse his mistakes. For European Christianity in the later nineteenth century was in full retreat before the rising tide of materialism and secularism. It had been profoundly weakened by centuries of sectarian strife, and tended to drift into a cultural backwater remote from the living movement of contemporary culture. Edmund Gosse's remarkable account of his father, the Victorian naturalist, in *Father and Son,* shows how the divorce between religion and the higher culture encouraged this form of religious escapism and isolated the believer in a sectarian group which absorbed his spiritual energies.[1] But this was not peculiar to Christianity, it was a symptom of the centrifugal character of nineteenth-century culture, and the artists, the men of letters and the social reformers and revolutionaries, including Nietzsche himself, all showed signs of the same attitude of withdrawal and all tended to form small closed groups and coteries in which they lived and worked. Certainly it was a way of escape, but what they were escaping from was not life, but the deadening pressure of the dominant secularized culture.

In so far, however, as sectarian Christianity involved, as in the case of Philip Gosse, an abdication of the Christian world mission and a deliberate limitation of its action for the benefit of a select minority, it involved a profound mis-

[1] This was not peculiar to Philip Gosse. One of the greatest men of science in the early nineteenth century, Faraday, was a member of a similar group, the Sandemanians.

understanding of the meaning of Christianity itself. Christianity began as a minority religion, a minority as small and obscure as any of the nineteenth-century sects. But at the same time, from the beginning it asserted its universal world-transforming mission, which embraced the whole history of the human race. It announced the coming of a new order in which mankind would be remade by the infusion of a higher spiritual principle. This original Christian conception of a new order must be distinguished from the "other-worldliness" characteristic of eighteenth- and nineteenth-century religion with its intense individualism and its preoccupation with emotional experience. For it was a cosmic process that was progressively realized in history and which made a new world by making a new humanity. It was essentially dynamic, as we see most clearly in St. Augustine's interpretation of history as a process of conflict between two conflicting wills and spiritual principles embodied in two opposing communities and social orders.

Thus Christian ethics are far more dynamic than Nietzsche realized. Indeed, in spite of the deliberately anti-Christian spirit and motive of his theory, there is a resemblance which almost suggests an element of unconscious imitation between his idea of the Superman and the transformation of culture by the discovery of a transcendent principle which creates new values, and the Christian idea of the New Man and the transformation of the present world order by the infusion of a new spiritual principle which creates a new morality and a new hierarchy of spiritual values. But if this is the real nature of Christianity, it is clear that the loss of the Christian faith and the Christian moral values has had a far more serious effect on European culture than Nietzsche believed, since what has been lost is not a negative morality which controlled the behaviour of the masses, but a transcendent spiritual end which gave Western culture its dynamic purpose. Of course this spiritual purpose and the moral values that it created were never completely realized in European culture, even in its most Christian development. But this is true of every religion and every ideology. Even in the lowest of them there is always a certain conflict and discrepancy between moral aims and social behaviour, and the gap is naturally widest where the religious faith and the moral aim is most transcendent. But this does not mean that religion does not affect culture. On the contrary, the more religious aims and moral values are recognized as transcendent, the more efficacious are they as a bond of union between different classes and communities. A secular ideology inevitably appeals to particular social interests and its moral values tend to be the values of a class or a nationality. But the moral values of a universal religion transcend their social limitations, so that Christianity was able to unite the slave and the freeman, the Roman citizen and the barbarian warrior, in the profession of the same faith, the communion of the same sacraments and the acceptance of the same moral standards and values.

These were the foundations on which Europe was built, and none of the great world cultures has owed more to the attractive and cohesive power of common religious beliefs and common moral aims. Consequently no culture has suffered more from the process of secularization, since as it proceeds it destroys all the common spiritual elements that have made Europe what it was and leaves only the conflicting forces of class and nationality and the social and scientific techniques which were the creation of the last phase of European culture. But no culture can survive by its technique alone. It is impossible for Europe to survive or to justify its existence merely as a successful "way of life" which produces more machinery, bigger bombs and more complicated gadgets than any other, for these things can be done better by the new world powers like America and Russia, powers which have far more favourable geographical and sociological conditions for the development of a unified mass civilization. Nor could the European problem be solved by a drastic process of economic and political reorganization which would create a federal unity—the United States of Europe—similar to the United States of America, for Europe possesses neither the common language nor the common political tradition which have played such an essential part in both the American and the Russian developments. The evils and exaggerations of modern nationalism must not blind us to the vital importance of nationality as an essential element in European culture. Europe owes its unique character to the fact that it is and always has been a society of nations, each intensely conscious of its own social personality and its own political institutions and laws, but all united by a common spiritual tradition, a common intellectual culture and common moral values. Even to-day in the present disintegrated state of European culture these common traditions and values are not altogether lost; they are weakened and undervalued, but they are not dead, and it is only by the recovery and strengthening of them that Europe can be saved.

Nor can it be said that these things have lost their importance in the new mechanized world. The advance of scientific technology may have made it possible to create calculating machines and mechanical "brains", but there will never be a machine for the creation of moral values. The last word in human affairs always belongs to the spiritual power that transcends both the order of nature and the order of culture and gives human life its ultimate meaning and purpose. It is only by the rediscovery of this power and the restoration of the triple relation between spiritual ends, moral values and social action that Europe can overcome its present cultural crisis, which is due above all to the growth of technical power and the loss of spiritual aim. This crisis is not confined to Europe, it is a universal problem that is common to the whole modern world. But it was in Europe that it first manifested itself, it is in Europe that it has assumed its most acute form, and it is Europe that possesses the greatest resources of knowledge and experience to deal with it. Therefore, in spite of Europe's material and political weakness, she is still in a position to decide the fate of the world by her victory or her defeat in these ultimate issues.

CHAPTER XII

The World Wars and the Growth of the Mass State

THE disintegration of European society by the forces of nationalism and the undermining of Western culture by the spiritual revolt of nihilism were gradual processes which continued for nearly two centuries without interfering with the material prosperity of our civilization or destroying the optimism and self-confidence of Western man. It was not until our own age that the situation was transformed by the catastrophe of the World Wars which suddenly destroyed the fools' paradise in which the peoples of Europe had been living and brought them face to face with the forces of destruction which had been accumulating beneath the surface of the modern world.

The First World War shook the foundations of our civilization. It ruined the economic predominance of Europe and destroyed for ever that sense of security and immunity from the extremes of physical suffering and the loss of personal freedom which had marked the civilization of the nineteenth century. Nevertheless it was not until the second war and the events of 1940 that we realized the extent to which we had been depending on illusions and the way in which the whole structure of European order could be destroyed by a single act of ruthless aggression.

Even so, the politicians and publicists of the West have clung to their illusions in spite of this terrible lesson. After each of the great wars they believed that victory would "make the world safe for democracy" and that they could set about planning a new world, a world of universal peace and prosperity with fair shares for all and equal rights for all peoples according to the ideals of liberal democracy.

But if history is any guide there is little reason to suppose that the new world which has passed through the fires of war will be a world of this kind. A great war is not a matter of human choice. On the contrary, it marks the point at which events pass out of human control. It is a kind of social convulsion—an eruption of the forces which lie dormant like the subterranean fires of a volcano on the slopes of which man builds his cities and cultivates his fields. If we look at any of the great wars of history—the Hundred Years War, the Thirty Years War, the Wars of the French Revolution —we see that their results are entirely different from anything that the leaders and statesmen who were responsible for them imagined or desired. And if this was the case with the pigmy wars of the past, waged by professional armies in a neat pattern of battles and sieges, how much more with the two World Wars that have overtaken us during the present generation—wars without shape or limit—total wars which absorb the entire effort of whole populations and affect the lives of hundreds of millions of men.

It was easy for the democratic politician to miss the real significance of what has befallen our civilization, and to explain the whole tragedy by attributing it to the moral obliquity of some particular guilty men—dictators or appeasers; so that when the war criminals had been eliminated civilization would go on its way as it had done before. But things are not so simple as that. Hitler and his like were not the creators of the world crisis, but its creatures who had been carried to power on the crest of the wave of destruction. Even Germany herself owed her importance to her weakness as much as to her strength. She was, as it were, the volcanic node where the spiritual fissures of our civilization intersected, the point at which the ordered surface of our society was broken through by the eruption of the subterranean forces.

Hence the activities of the modern planners and international reformers bear the same relation to the world crisis as the activities of a mining engineer or even a plumber to a volcanic eruption. They are sensible and rational and scientific, but they belong to an essentially different plane from that of the forces which they are attempting to master. The foundations of our world are shaken and we shall not save it by replanning the superstructure.

What, then, is the real nature of the problem?

An immense material and technical revolution has taken place which has entirely changed the conditions of human life without any corresponding change in human nature. The revolution has been the work of a minority—of a few men in a few societies—but the results of it affect everybody and they are being progressively adopted and applied by all societies to all men. The result is that there has been no time to train man in the use of his new powers. We take the peasant from his bullock-wagon and teach him to drive an automobile, then we teach him to drive a tank or an aeroplane, and before he realizes what has happened—while his mind is still unconsciously embedded in the folk ways of his peasant ancestors—he finds himself a unit in a mass that is being irresistibly impelled forwards in a race of industrial production or military destruction, which he is powerless to understand or control.

This rapidity of change, this sudden diffusion of the achievements of modern science and technology, was welcomed by the nineteenth century as an absolute good— as the advance of progress and enlightenment at the expense of ignorance and barbarism. And it was especially welcomed by liberal opinion in Western Europe and America as an essentially democratic process—the practical realization of the principle of equality and the rights of the common man. It was only by degrees that men began to realize that the change in social scale caused by the unlimited extension of industrial and scientific techniques also involved a serious threat to democracy, and even to-day the lesson has not been fully learned. For while mass society is favourable to democracy in so far as it destroys hereditary privilege and traditional authority and represents a general tendency towards uniformity and equalization, at the same time it is hostile to freedom, since it reduces the control of the individual over his own life and makes him the instrument of collective forces on which his very existence depends. The fathers of the democratic tradition—English squires like Hampden and Cromwell and Vane, Virginian planters like Washington and Jefferson, New England lawyers and publicists like the Adamses and Benjamin Franklin—were all of them very highly conscious of the importance of the individual personality as the ultimate and indestructible social value. They regarded the state as the servant and guarantee of their individual rights, and in so far as they envisaged the advance of science and economic organization they looked on them as opening a wider field for individual initiative, not as creating an organization by which the life of the individual would be standardized and controlled.

But the situation was utterly different when the movement passed to societies that knew nothing of this tradition of personal freedom, societies in which human life was cheap, where the individual was nothing and the state and the masters of the state were everything. So long as the new techniques were the monopoly of the same peoples who had produced the individualist culture, as was the case throughout the greater part of the nineteenth century, the difficulty did not arise: liberty, democracy, and scientific technique were allies. But as soon as the movement had become world-wide, when the era of the masses had begun, it became clear that liberty and scientific efficiency were not necessarily united. The societies which had no experience of, or respect for, freedom were in some ways better adapted to scientific mass organization than those which put the rights of the individual first. And it was here that the German development acquired such crucial importance, since it was in Germany that the new scientific techniques were first harnessed and controlled by a centralized military state. Already in the eighteenth century Prussia had gone further than any earlier state in the scientific organization of its people for war, and the drill sergeants of Frederick the Great had solved in advance the problem of how to convert a multitude of individuals with different temperaments and degrees of intelligence into a mass machine which could be manipulated with automatic precision by a single mind and will.

This mass conditioning of the Prussian people two centuries ago not only made a profound impression on the national character and tradition, but also provided a pattern of military and bureaucratic efficiency which was accepted by the other peoples of Central and Eastern Europe, above all by Russia, whose German rulers showed a marked preference for German men and German methods in the administration of their empire.

In the course of the nineteenth century these military empires gradually divested themselves of their feudal and theocratic elements; until, with the First World War, the moment came when the dynasties themselves collapsed and the mass organization of the state was brought into direct and immediate relation with the mass organism of the people.

This was the origin of the phenomenon which we call the Totalitarian State—a system which can be called democratic inasmuch as it represents the rule of the masses, but which is entirely hostile to the ideals of freedom and humanity and the rights of the individual citizen which are inseparable from the democratic tradition as we have always understood it in the West.

We must, however, face the fact that the mass state can be no less efficient than the free state and that in certain respects it is even better adapted to the new scale and tempo due to the universal extension of modern scientific techniques. Moreover, at the same time that these new Leviathans were growing up in the East, Western democracy was itself following a parallel development towards mass organization. Democratic parties, the democratic press and the democratic organization of labour have acquired a very different character from that which they possessed a century ago. They no longer offer the same field for open discussion and free individual initiative. The statesman who speaks to a constituency of sixty or seventy millions is dealing with a situation which is qualitatively and not merely quantitatively different from that which existed in the early days of liberal democracy. And the same is true of the industrialist or labour leader who no longer has to deal with the competition of individuals, but with anonymous economic masses whose behaviour must be studied with the scientific detachment of an astronomer or a meteorologist. Our Western ideas of political and economic freedom, our concepts of free speech and government by discussion, our ideas of property and wealth and leisure, even our ideals of education and culture, were all framed under different conditions in a different society. They come from an age when states numbered a few million inhabitants and a few hundred thousand politically active citizens. It is only with difficulty that they can maintain themselves in a world that has become a single power area—where states number their populations by the hundred million and where the whole of their populations are standardized by the same techniques and the pressure of the same economic forces.

Yet it is clear that we cannot abandon ourselves to the forces of change with the same optimistic faith with which our ancestors welcomed the age of progress. No one who is loyal to the spirit of Western civilization, whether in America or Europe, can accept the ethics of the totalitarian state, with its denial of human rights, its mass executions, and its ruthless liquidation of minorities, without moral disintegration. We are bound in honour not only to fight this evil abroad, but to prevent our own society following the same path.

And, as I have said, we cannot do this by economic planning, essential as that may be; because the mass state thrives on planning hardly less than on war. The real evil lies deeper—in the breach that has taken place between the technical development of our civilization and its spiritual life. In the last resort every civilization is built on a religious foundation: it is the expression in social institutions and cultural activity of a faith or a vision of reality which gives the civilization its spiritual unity. Thus the great world cultures correspond with the great world religions, and when a religion dies the civilization that it has inspired gradually decays. "Where there is no vision, the people perish."

We do not recognize this more clearly because of the difference in time-scale between the individual human life and the life of a civilization, so that the ordinary man is only aware of an infinitesimal aspect of the process of which he forms a part. When we speak of a civilization being secular or materialist, it does not mean that that civilization possesses no spiritual basis; it means that civilization has become temporarily extroverted and that its attention is concentrated on the practical aspects that lie on the surface of its consciousness.

This is what has happened in the case of our own civilization. There has never been a society so totally absorbed in the technique and equipment of civilization or more neglectful of the ultimate spiritual values for the sake of which the human race exists.

The civilizations of the past devoted a greater part of their slender resources to the service of these ultimate values than we can afford with our wealth and power. Chartres and Amiens are as marvellous feats of material construction as any modern skyscraper or industrial plant. But whereas the latter exist only to serve a temporary need, the former express the very heart and soul of the culture. If a civilization is entirely concentrated on external activity, on techniques and mechanics, on means as distinct from ends, its gain in material power and control over nature is counterbalanced by a loss of harmony, a loss of balance between the inner and the outer worlds of experience, which causes it to exhaust its reserves of spiritual power and makes it brittle and unstable.

We have a terrible object lesson of this before our eyes in the fate of modern Germany. No society devoted itself more successfully to the cult of technocracy, none accomplished greater feats of scientific organization. But it failed entirely to preserve its inner harmony and to protect the spiritual values which gave civilization its ultimate justification. It became the blind servant of the will to power. And the result was that the social machine got out of control and the scientists and the technologists became the servants and the slaves of the Party that made the strongest appeal to the crudest and most elementary mass emotions. Now, owing to the reasons that I have already discussed, the German people is peculiarly predisposed to this kind of mass suggestion, especially when it is associated with the cult of military power. But, apart from this, the same problem exists for the whole of modern civilization, and we are none of us immune from these dangers, though they present themselves to us in less violent and shocking forms. But everywhere we see the same tendency to extroversion, the same depreciation of spiritual values and the same weakening of spiritual vitality.

In our case it has been the war of business and not the business of war that has absorbed our energies: a better and more human alternative, we may say, but one which is no less far removed from the ultimate vision of reality, from what the makers of Europe, and the makers of America also, regarded as the true life—*vita beata*. For our civilization, like all the other great civilizations of the world, has its religious foundation, and its exceptional achievements are ultimately due to the dynamism of its religious impulse. This impulse still makes itself felt in modern civilization, and it is impossible to understand many of the most representative modern statesmen and thinkers unless we recognize the influence, both conscious and unconscious, of this spiritual tradition that unites them with the original source of Western culture.

If we regard our civilization as an organic whole and not merely in its local and temporary manifestations, we shall see that it contains unsuspected depths of spiritual power and knowledge. The immense extension of our civilization in space and time, together with its increase in material wealth and technical achievement, has undoubtedly led us away from our spiritual centre and has weakened or destroyed our sense of spiritual community. It would be foolish to underestimate the extent of this divorce of our modern civilization from its vital spiritual foundations. It is the malady of our age, and, as we see from its results in Germany, it may well be fatal to the society that gives way to it completely. But there is no reason to believe that the disease is irresistible or incurable. The deeper levels of human consciousness have not been lost by the changes of the last hundred years: they have only been obscured and overlaid by surface activities. The recovery of our civilization is therefore above all a question of restoring the balance between its inner and outer life. The unlimited material expansion of our civilization has weakened it by making it superficial, and the time has come for a movement in the reverse direction—a movement of concentration to recover its inner strength and unity. No doubt it is extremely difficult to bring this need home to the average citizen who is immersed in the practical task of earning his living or in the specialized techniques of scientific organization; for in proportion as a culture becomes secularized it no longer possesses a common language to express its deepest needs. Thus if we state the need in the traditional religious language, it is dismissed as pious platitudes or theological abstractions, while if we use the language of philosophy, we address ourselves to a small minority that has little contact with the culture of modern mass society.

In the past the popular culture of both the English and American peoples was based on the Bible; that is to say, the greatest religious literature in the world was the common possession of the common people. God and the soul, salvation and damnation, the Word and the Spirit, were concepts which formed the background to the ordinary man's view of the world and of history. But to-day, when the cinema and the picture paper have taken the place of the Church and the Bible as the source of popular culture, it is obviously far more difficult to find a pathway from the surface world of specialized work and mechanized amusement to the deeper level of reality on which the life of our civilization depends.

In the present generation, however, the situation has been profoundly changed by the impact of war. The old world of careless security, private liberty and growing material prosperity has been blown and blasted to bits by two World Wars, and the rise of the new mass society that has arisen upon its ruins is changing the whole pattern of social life. Everywhere the threat of the totalitarian state and the prestige of the totalitarian ideal of a planned economy have led to a great change in the balance of power between the state and the individual and to the narrowing or elimination of that margin of freedom thanks to which the higher forms of culture have been able to grow and bear fruit.

The inclement climate of this post-war world is unfavourable not only to the economic and political privileges of favoured classes and individuals but to the privileged position of those societies which have hitherto enjoyed an exceptional status in the world.

But there are more important questions than these. If Europe is forced to surrender its old position of political and economic hegemony, it is all the more important to maintain the spiritual foundations on which our culture has been built and without which it cannot preserve its identity.

It is here that the conflict with the power of the mass society and the totalitarian world state becomes most acute. For the new powers are not content with controlling the external side of social life by political organization and economic planning: they seek to rule men's minds also, and to control their thoughts and wills by the techniques of mass conditioning and psychological pressure. Thus they are the enemies not only of the democratic Rights of Man and the humanist ideals of personality and nationality, but still more of those fundamental spiritual principles which are inseparable from the Christian faith and which have been the foundation of the whole development of Western culture. Wherever the totalitarian state is dominant it is forced by its nature to become a persecuting power. We saw this on a small scale in Nazi Germany and we now see it developed far more systematically and on a far larger scale throughout the Communist world. This is not religious persecution as we have known it in the past. The old forms of persecution were for the most part episodes in a conflict between rival religions. They relied on the simple weapons of intimidation and physical pressure so that the freedom of choice remained even though it might be the choice of a cruel death. But the martyr, the man who resisted to blood, was regarded by his fellows and sometimes by his opponents as a witness to a power that was greater than that of the state and stronger than death itself. Thus in the great conflict between Christianity and the world power of the Roman Empire it was by the blood of the martyrs that the Church gained the victory. The martyrs became the hero-founders of the new Christian world, and even to-day their memory is kept alive in thousands of shrines and temples in every European land.

But the new form of persecution is inspired by different motives and makes use of new and more formidable weapons than were known in the past. It leaves no room for the prestige of martyrdom: indeed it is directed with inhuman patience and persistence against the very spirit of martyrdom itself. Persecution as we see it to-day culminates not in the martyr's witness and his glorious death, but in a public confession and act of self-accusation, which is intended to discredit him and his cause; after which he is quietly liquidated or consigned to the living death of a concentration camp.

In the use of these methods, Communist totalitarianism has already gone much further than the Nazis, and a long series of state trials has shown that the normal human personality is incapable of resisting the pressure that can be brought to bear upon it by the new techniques of Communist "justice".

This is a disquieting fact for Christians who have always looked to the witness of the martyrs as the ultimate proof of the unconquerable strength of their faith. But it is not a problem for Christians alone, for the totalitarian threat to freedom involves every aspect of human life. The techniques of mass conditioning and psychological control operate at every level, from their beginnings in the crude methods of political slogans and Party purges to their culmination in the elaborate psychological techniques which subdue the will and conscience of the individual and force the thinker and the religious leader to denounce their friends and deny their convictions.

Now it is not surprising that the new mass societies should have discovered methods unknown in a more individualistic type of society to weaken or destroy the autonomy of the individual mind, and to make it accept passively the beliefs and suggestions that are backed with the weight of social authority. Joseph de Maistre wrote long ago of the French Revolution that the lightest opinion of the revolutionary party was like a battering-ram with twenty million wills behind it, and now that the mass society has become scientifically organized as a vast machine of power which embraces a hundred million lives, it is inevitable that it must overcome the resistance of even the strongest individual will, if the latter is confronted, not with an impersonal law administered by an impartial institution as in the Western tradition, but with an organized mass which corresponds psychologically to the unified physical mass power of a disciplined army.

There can unfortunately be no doubt that as the development of scientific techniques has increased the destructiveness of modern war, so also it has immeasurably increased the dangers of tyranny, when the tyranny is exercised not by an arbitrary despot but by a scientifically organized bureaucratic police state. This is no longer a hypothetical problem; it has become the condition under which a large part of the human race exists to-day. In Western Europe and America we have hitherto been slow to recognize this danger, owing to the fact that our whole approach to science and technology has been coloured by the optimism and idealism of Liberal democracy. But now that the privileged position of Western Europe has been lost, we are obliged to face the facts of mass civilization in a spirit of sober realism. We cannot hope to escape the ordeal of the peoples of Eastern Europe merely because we have hitherto enjoyed a much greater measure of social liberty and freedom of thought. On the other hand we cannot accept the principle of totalitarian organization with all its psychological and spiritual consequences without denying everything for which Europe has stood hitherto, and thus destroying the very essence and identity of our culture.

We cannot resist the pressure of totalitarianism by external means alone. Military rearmament and economic reorganization, however necessary they may be, will not save us since they are themselves part of the impersonal process that is creating the mass society. Nor is it possible to rely on the uncoordinated efforts of free individuals, for, as we have seen, the unsupported human will is incapable of resisting the psychological pressure of an organized mass power.

The only remaining solution is a reintegration of Western culture which will recover the spiritual resources which have been neglected during the triumphant material expansion of the last century, but which still remain dormant yet not extinct under the surface of our extroverted and divided society. Such a regeneration of our civilization demands a concentration of our spiritual energies and resources such as we can hardly conceive at present. The Churches and the universities, which are the traditional guardians of these resources, have suffered—especially in the English-speaking world—from the same tendency to extroversion and superficial activity, which has been the general weakness of our age and our civilization.

The recovery of spiritual unity and the integration of life on the deeper level of consciousness cannot be achieved in a moment by a deliberate social act. That is why war and social revolution, which yield quick results—of a kind—appeal more to human nature than the more fundamental process of social and spiritual renewal, the results of which are not immediately visible. Nevertheless it is no longer possible to regard this process of social regeneration as either impossible or unnecessary.

The old conventions regarding the limits of practical politics, and the relation of politics and business and of public and private interests, have been destroyed by the combined influence of totalitarianism and technocracy. The new techniques of mass power and social control cannot be abolished or forgotten, even if their misuse can be checked. We are faced with the choice between social regimentation and social regeneration, and if we do not possess the vision and the patience to realize the latter we shall inevitably be forced to adopt the former, in the same way as we have been forced to adopt the regimentation of total war in our opposition to the totalitarian state.

The continued existence of European civilization depends on whether the Western peoples are capable of dealing seriously and realistically with this fundamental issue. Social regeneration or spiritual renewal is not just a high-sounding phrase which can be left to preachers and moralists; it is the basic sociological problem of our time. For unless we find a way to restore the contact between the life of society and the life of the spirit our civilization will be destroyed by the forces which it has had the knowledge to create but not wisdom to control.

CHAPTER XIII

The Problem of the Future:
Total Secularization or a Return to Christian Culture

WE have seen that the weakness of Western culture in face of the new forces that threaten its existence is due above all to its loss of faith in its own spiritual values and the growing detachment of its external way of life from its religious foundations and the sources of its spiritual vitality. If Europe is to survive—if we do not surrender to the inhuman ideal of a mass society which is a mere engine of the will to power—we must find some way to reverse this process and to recover our spiritual unity.

This is a problem of re-education in the widest sense of the word. For, as I pointed out in the first chapter, the secularization of modern culture is inseparably connected with the secularization of modern education and the passing of control from the Church and the old teaching corporations to the modern state. The old system stood in grievous need of reform. The misfortune was that the necessary reform was carried out in a narrowly utilitarian spirit with no awareness of the deeper spiritual and psychological factors that were involved. The result was that the modern world has been inundated by a shallow flood of universal literacy which destroyed the old traditions of popular culture and increased the mass-mindedness of modern society without raising its cultural standards or deepening its spiritual life.

No doubt this expansion of universal primary instruction is only one side of modern education. On the other side, there has been the advance of scientific research and the development of the new scientific techniques which have transformed the external conditions of human life. But all the achievements of modern science have been powerless to restore the broken unity of our culture. Indeed the progress of scientific specialization is itself one of the causes of the centrifugal and divided character of modern civilization. Neither in science nor elsewhere in the modern world do we see the emergence of any power which is capable of performing the essential function that religion has hitherto fulfilled in the societies of the past as a principle of cultural unity and as the creator of moral values.

Taken in its widest sense education is simply the process by which the new members of a community are initiated into its ways of life and thought from the simplest elements of behaviour or manners up to the highest tradition of spiritual wisdom. Christian education is therefore an initiation into the Christian way of life and thought, and for one thousand two hundred years, more or less, the peoples of Europe have been submitted to this influence. The process has been intensive at some points, superficial at others, but taking it as a whole it may be said that nowhere else in the history of mankind can we see such a mighty stream of intellectual and moral effort directed through so many channels to a single end. However incomplete its success may have been, there is no doubt that it has changed the world, and no one has any right to talk of the history of Western civilization unless he has done his best to understand its aims and its methods.

But on the whole men have not done so. It has been neglected both by the historians and by the educationalists, who have tended to approach their subjects from a different point of view. It is true that a treatment of history which is openly hostile to or contemptuous of Christian culture, like that of Gibbon, is usually regarded as biased, but it is quite possible to write of European culture as of national history, leaving the Christian tradition entirely out of the picture, without the average reader's realizing that anything is missing. Nevertheless it was, as we have seen, that tradition that conditioned the whole development of culture from the fifth to the nineteenth century and which created the standards of value and the vision or reality which inspired its most characteristic achievements. To-day religious education is apt to be considered a kind of extra, insecurely tacked on to the general educational structure, not unlike a Gothic church in a modern housing estate. But in the past it was the foundation on which the whole edifice of culture was based and which was deeply embedded below the surface of social consciousness.

For from the beginning Christian education was conceived not so much as learning a lesson but as introduction into a new life, or still more as an initiation into a mystery. The early manuals of Christian education, like the Catechetical Discourses of St. Cyril or the *De Catechizandis Rudibus* of St. Augustine, all stress the esoteric character of the teaching. For example, at the beginning of St. Cyril of Jerusalem's Discourses we read the following notice: "These Catechetical Lectures thou mayest put into the hands of candidates for Baptism and of baptised believers, but by no means of Catechumens nor of any others who are not Christians as thou shalt answer to the Lord. And if thou takest a copy of them write this in the beginning, as in the sight of the Lord." Christian education was something that could not be conveyed by words alone, but which involved a discipline of the whole man; a process of catharsis and illumination which centred in the sacred mysteries, and which was embodied in a cycle of symbolism and liturgical action.

Thus Christian education was not only an initiation into the Christian community, it was also an initiation into *another world*: the unveiling of spiritual realities of which the natural man was unaware and which changed the meaning of existence. And I think it is here that our modern education—including our religious education—has proved defective. There is in it no sense of *revelation*. It is accepted as instruction, sometimes as useful knowledge, often as tiresome task work in preparation for some examination, but nowhere do we find that joyful sense of the discovery of a new and wonderful reality which inspired true Christian culture. All true religious teaching leads up to the contemplation of divine mysteries, and where this is lacking, the whole culture becomes weakened and divided. It may be objected that this is the sphere of worship and not of education; but it is impossible to separate the two, since it was largely in the sphere of worship that the Christian tradition of education and culture arose and developed. The first Christian education was the initiation into the divine mysteries in the liturgical sense, and it brought with it a development of religious poetry and music and art which was the first-fruits of Christian culture.

It is perhaps difficult for us to appreciate the educational significance of this, because the Christian liturgy and its associated literature and art are still accepted as a living element in our contemporary religious life, so that we do not at once realize how different is the position it holds in our culture from that which it held in the past.

At the present day, the Church is but one institution amongst a whole series of cultural organs which compete with one another to form public opinion—the cinema and the wireless, drama and fiction, the press and the advertisement industry, not to mention the youth movements and the political parties. But in the past, for whole centuries and especially for the common people, the Church covered the whole orbit of culture and it was only in the Church that the ordinary man found instruction, inspiration and spiritual sustenance. The churches still stand as the most striking objects in the European landscape, whether they dominate the cities, like Chartres and Lincoln, or whether they are lost in the countryside, like the village churches of England. But in either case, they are monuments of a vanished age and culture, and they are no longer the vital centres of the community to which they belong. We must see them as they were in the days of their glory, glowing with colour, rich with sculpture, and filled with the music and dramatic action of the liturgy—power-houses of the spirit—to realize the place they once held in the life of a people, which was in other respects far poorer than it is to-day. Yet even to-day the churches in their comparatively derelict condition are by no means negligible in their influence on culture. To quote my own experience, I learnt more during my school-days from my visits to the Cathedral at Winchester than I did from the hours of religious instruction in school. That great church with its tombs of the Saxon kings and the mediaeval statesmen-bishops gave one a greater sense of the magnitude of the religious element in our culture and the depths of its roots in our national life than anything one could learn from books. Nor was it merely a question of widening one's historical sense, it also deepened one's spiritual sense of religion as an objective reality far transcending one's private experience. And if this can be so even to-day, how much more in the past when the cult of the saints and the holy places consecrated the whole historical and geographical context of culture and gave every social relation and activity its appropriate religious symbolism.

In Northern Europe this accumulated treasure of religious symbolism was dispersed by the Reformation, which destroyed the liturgical character of popular culture and at the same time caused a great breach in the historical continuity of Christian tradition. Nevertheless it did not by any means undervalue the importance of religious education. On the contrary, the Reformers regarded their work largely as a reform or restoration of Christian education, which corresponded on the religious side to the renaissance of classical learning on the part of the humanists. Back to the Bible, the Bible only and the Bible for all; these were the slogans of the new religious education which so profoundly affected English culture in the sixteenth and seventeenth centuries. And this involved important changes of psychological approach. It emphasized the literary element in education at the expense of the æsthetic, and it increased the importance of the individual as against the community. Wherever the Protestant tradition of education had free play—in Scotland, Holland, England, Geneva and New England for example—it had a marked effect in increasing the literacy of the common people and in developing individualism, moral activism and independence of judgment, though this was paid for by losses in other directions which showed themselves in the growing impoverishment of the communal life of society.

Volumes may be written on the social consequences of this divergence between the two traditions of Christian education—the liturgical Catholic and the Biblical Protestant. But they have not been written, so far as I am aware, and even in the discussions that have arisen on the possibility of an agreed syllabus of religious education, this aspect of the question has been little regarded. The divergence was no doubt to some extent reduced by the strong influence of humanist education on Catholic and Protestant alike. Moreover, the two traditions influenced one another even at the period when religious disagreement was sharpest. Thus the catechism, which from the sixteenth century almost to the present day was the regular method of religious instruction, was of Protestant origin, but has become no less characteristic of modern Catholic religious education, while from the other side the Jesuit system of education exercised a considerable influence on Protestant grammar-schools and academies.

But if the combined influence of Renaissance and Reformation made for the wider diffusion of literary culture and the intellectualizing of religious education, it also tended to increase the practical and utilitarian elements of culture. Both the Byzantine East and the mediaeval West had shared the same ideal of contemplation and spiritual vision as the supreme end and justification of all human culture: an ideal which finds classical expression in St. Thomas and Dante. But from the fifteenth century onwards culture and education became increasingly concerned with the claims of active life. The humanist ideal of an all-round cultivation of man's physical and intellectual abilities was brought into relation with the Protestant ideal of what Troeltsch has called secular or *innerweltlich* ascetism—of sanctification by the diligent exercise of man's "calling"—of doing his duty in the state of life in which it has pleased God to call him. And this in turn led to the cultivation of the economic virtues of thrift and industry and to the acquisition of "useful knowledge" as the main end of education. There can be no doubt that secular utilitarianism was the direct product and heir of the religious utilitarianism that developed on the soil of Protestant, and specifically of Puritan, culture: for though Bentham himself was a disciple of the French Enlightenment, he was but the rationalizer of the movement, and its most characteristic types are a real native product of Protestant culture.

Now while this tradition, which we may call the tradition of Samuel Smiles, generated a great force of moral and practical energy, it was also responsible for the harsh and unattractive character of modern culture. One of the greatest Victorian educationalists—Matthew Arnold—was never tired of insisting on this, and unlike most of his modern successors, he was not afraid to trace it back to its theological roots. "The period which is now ending for England", he wrote, "is that which began when, after the sensuous tumult of the Renaissance, Catholicism being discredited and gone, our serious nature desired, as had been foretold, to see one of the days of the Son of Man and did not see it, but men said to them: see here and see there, and they went after the blind guides and followed the false direction, and the actual civilization of England and America is the result. A civilization with many virtues, but without lucidity of mind and without largeness of temper. And now we English, at any rate, have to acquire them, and to learn the necessity for us, 'to live (as Emerson says) from a greater depth of being'. The sages and the saints alike have always preached this necessity; the so-called practical people and men of the world have always derided it. In the present collapse of this wisdom we ought to find it less hard to rate their stock ideas and stock phrases, their claptrap and their catchwords at their proper value, and to cast in our lot boldly with the sages and with the saints"[1]. Arnold preached this doctrine indefatigably to Mid-Victorian England, and he was in an exceptionally favourable position to influence educational policy, since for thirty-five years he was an official of the Education Department and was appointed again and again as assistant commissioner to the royal commissions that were appointed to consider educational policy. Yet I do not think it can be said that his

[1] Preface to *Irish Essays* (1882).

influence was great on the thing that mattered most and on which he was most right, namely the spiritual foundation of culture. Not only so, but he was himself in part responsible for the general unpopularity and bad odour into which the idea of culture has fallen in this country. For Matthew Arnold was what is now known as a high-brow. He was indeed the original and archetypal high-brow, and the war he declared against the enemies of culture was ultimately followed by that reaction against culture and that Philistine reign of terror under which we live to-day.

The fact is that culture by itself—even a humanist culture that is intellectually aware of the spiritual values of Christianity—does not possess the power of restoring or transforming the life of society. It provides standards of value, intellectual and æsthetic appreciation, the development of the power of criticism, width of knowledge and detachment from the prejudices and errors both of the multitude and of the ruling class. All this Arnold had—like his contemporaries Renan and Sainte-Beuve in France, or Emerson and Henry James and Henry Adams in America, all of them superior people who stood aside on their intellectual eminence and watched the stream of life go by. They none of them had the religious attitude to life, though they all realized how important it was to have it. They lacked faith and therefore they lacked charity and therefore they failed to gain men's sympathies and even aroused conscious or unconscious antagonism.

This is why the utilitarians, the apostles of useful knowledge and applied science, have been their superiors in the educational field, though their views were often so much more narrow and superficial. They had a simple naïve faith in the value of concrete objective knowledge which they communicated to others. And this created a bond of sympathy between utilitarian high-brows like Bentham and Mill and hard-headed practical men like Francis Place.

In the past, in a Christian society, the leaders of culture were just as critical of the views and behaviour of common humanity as were the modern humanists. But even the most high-brow of Christian teachers such as Pascal and Newman stood on common ground with the common people before the supreme mystery of faith.

> God of Abraham, God of Isaac, God of Jacob
> Not of the philosophers and men of learning
>   God of Jesus Christ
> Deum meum et Deum vestrum.

The mystery of faith brings all men together at the heart of life, and it reduces the differences of culture, in the humanist sense of the word, to comparative insignificance.

Faith is therefore the beginning and end of Christian culture as it is the beginning and end of Christian morals. This is common to all forms of Christianity, Catholic, Orthodox, and Protestant; only in so far as the conception of faith differs is there also a difference in the conception of culture. Indeed I do not think it is too far-fetched to suggest that the essential difference between the Catholic and Protestant conceptions of the relation of religion and culture is bound up with their respective conceptions of the relation of faith and works, the famous controversy which above all others divided the Churches at the Reformation. For just as the Catholics taught that there was a vital, organic, inseparable relation between faith and works, as against the Protestant view of justification by faith alone, so too in the Catholic view there is an organic relation between religion and culture, which the Protestant view does not as a rule recognize. And this I think is one of the main causes for that indifference of modern Protestantism to culture, which was the burden of Matthew Arnold's controversial writings —the grimness and greyness of certain aspects of English and American life in the nineteenth century and the indifference of the most religious sections of English and American society to the cause of higher education.

To-day this is a thing of the past. The harsh and ugly sub-culture of Victorian industrialism with its combination of unlimited acquisitiveness with narrow pietism, has no defenders, and the reaction against Puritanism has carried England and the U.S.A. to the opposite extreme of an extroverted hedonistic mass culture. But some things have been carried over from one extreme to the other without much change, and the most important of these are the contempt for ideas and the indifference to humane culture, which are hardly less characteristic of the mass man of to-day than of the individualistic Philistines of yesterday. The latter, even though they were themselves men of genuine religious faith and moral earnestness, were the destroyers of the Christian tradition of culture, and their successors have filled the void with a materialist pseudo-culture which is the real opium of the people, since it is at once a drug and an intoxicant and a poison.

For modern civilization to-day seems to be following the same road as the ancient world under the Roman Empire; on the one hand, a vast development of material resources and luxury—above all luxury for the masses—bread and games and baths and theatres; on the other, the vast development of power—the overwhelming pressure of unlimited power, concentrated in the hands of the masters of the world. But in our case the danger is greater, because our power and resources are incomparably greater, and because the tradition we are losing is not that of the pagan city-state, but that of Christendom. Nevertheless this gloomy parallel is not altogether a hopeless one. For the decline of the classical culture and the growth of the massive power of the world state did not actually produce in the long run a materialist culture. It was followed by a sudden escape of humanity into a new spiritual dimension, the discovery of a new spiritual world and the acquisition of a new spiritual freedom. It was the age of Tiberius and Nero that saw the coming of Christianity, and the breakdown of the giant fabric of the world state in the third century was followed by the rise of the new Christian culture.

The present crisis of our civilization can only be solved by a similar process of radical conversion and spiritual transformation. Hard as it may be to see the possibility of this, it is no less difficult to believe in the possibility of indefinite progress along the present line to some robot utopia. Indeed the catastrophes of the last thirty years are not only a sign of the bankruptcy of secular humanism, they also go to show that a completely secularized civilization is inhuman in the absolute sense—hostile to human life and irreconcilable with human nature itself. For as I have tried to explain in *The Judgement of the Nations,* the forces of violence and aggressiveness that threaten to destroy our world are the direct result of the starvation and frustration of man's spiritual nature. For a time Western civilization managed to live on the normal tradition of the past, maintained by a kind of sublimated humanitarian idealism. But this was essentially a transitional phenomenon, and as humanism and humanitarianism fade away, we see societies more and more animated by the blind will to power which drives them on to destroy one another and ultimately themselves. Civilization can only be creative and life-giving in the proportion that it is spiritualized. Otherwise the increase of power inevitably increases its power for evil and its destructiveness.

Therefore it is only by the rediscovery of the spiritual world and the restoration of man's spiritual capacities that it is possible to save humanity from self-destruction. This is the immense task which Christian education has to undertake. It involves a great deal more than any Christian or any educationalist has yet realized. And this is inevitable because we are dealing with unknown factors which lie beyond our horizon of vision, below our level of consciousness and above the capacity of our reason: in other words the problem concerns the future, the human soul and God: three things which we cannot understand. For this reason, modern man, who has been accustomed to living in a world which is scientifically known and technologically controlled, is in a worse position for dealing with the ultimate religious problems than his ancestors, who were at every turn faced with mysterious forces over which they had no control and who consequently felt an obvious immediate, practical sense of dependence on the power and assistance of God.

But this does not mean that we ought to acquiesce, as some modern Christian thinkers are inclined to do, in the complete incomprehensibility and otherness of Faith—in a dualism of religion and culture which leaves no room for Christian education. The greater is our knowledge of nature and man and history, the greater is the obligation to use these increased resources for God, not merely in the way of moral action, but intellectually also, by the re-interpretation of the tradition of Christian culture in terms of the new knowledge, and by relating the instruments of culture to their true spiritual end.

At the present time there is a great danger that the part of culture should be undervalued and neglected both in the religious and the educational spheres. In the latter there is a tendency to sacrifice the humanities to science and technology; in the former there is the theological dualism to which I have just referred, which finds its most striking expression in the Barthian return to the theology of Luther and Calvin presented in a new dialectical form. Both these tendencies in their different ways are unfavourable to the traditional Christian culture and to the old discipline of studies which was conceived as an ascending scale of humanity, philosophy and divinity. The disintegration of higher education into a mass of divergent speculations co-ordinated only by motives of economic and political interest is fatal to any ideal of culture, and if, as is sometimes the case, religious knowledge is treated as one of these independent specialisms, it is even more fatal to religion. The recovery of a Christian culture is therefore the essential educational and religious task, and it is inseparable from the social ideal of Christendom—of the Christian people—*plebs Christiana—populus Dei*. This ideal which has become so pale and remote to the individualism and secularism of the nineteenth century, and indeed of the whole modern world, lies at the very heart of Christianity. It was equally present in the Middle Ages when Christendom was a triumphant world culture and in the days when Christianity was a persecuted underground movement, but when nevertheless Christians were conscious of being a new people, "a third race" on whose heads the ends of the world were come.

If from the standpoint of the Roman man of the world, these Christians were an uneducated lot of barbarians, we must remember that they were in reality just as much the heirs of a tradition of culture as the cultivated Hellenist, and that they brought into the tired and sophisticated civilization of the Roman Empire the accumulated treasures of a profound spiritual experience which was on a different plane of reality from anything that Greece and Rome had known. And in the modern world there is a similar tradition of sacred culture which it has been the mission of the Church to nourish and preserve. However secularized our modern civilization may become, this sacred tradition remains like a river in the desert, and a genuine religious education can still use it to irrigate the thirsty lands and to change the face of the world with the promise of new life. The great obstacle is the failure of Christians themselves to understand the depth of that tradition and the inexhaustible possibilities of new life that it contains.

INDEX